CRYSTALS
THE JOURNEY BEGINS
——ARE YOU COMING?——

A personal journey into the crystal kingdom by Bryan Gardiner

CRYSTALS: The Journey Begins - Are You Coming?

by

Bryan S. Gardiner

ISBN Number 0 646 12588 5

Published by Adrona Pty Ltd 2/191 Riversdale Road,
Hawthorn. Victoria, 3122 Australia. ACN 006 838 026
Postal Address: P. O. Box 6666, St. Kilda Road Central,
Victoria, 3004 Australia.

First Published - April 1993.
Reprinted May 1994.
Reprinted December 1995 - minor updates.
Illustration and Design - Julie Ann Malcolm

Distribution:
Australia: Gemcraft Books, (03) 9888 0111
United States: New Leaf Distributing Company, (770) 948 7845
Printed by McPhersons Printing Group, Victoria, Australia.

CONTENTS

1. My Introduction to Crystals   **6**

LET'S SET THE SCENE   6

WHERE DO WE START   11

MY FIRST STEP   13

MY SECOND STEP   14

MY THIRD STEP   17

MY FOURTH STEP   18

MY DIRECTION CLARIFIED   20

HOW I ARRIVED AT THIS POINT   23

WHERE TO NOW?   25

2. Some Background Information On: **28**

CRYSTAL & MINERALS - DEFINITIONS   28

HISTORY OF CRYSTALS   29

MASTER HEALERS   33

GETTING YOUR OWN CRYSTALS/GEMS   35

CRYSTALS AND GEMS -CLEANSING   36

PROGRAMMING CRYSTALS   40

CHAKRA POINTS & BALANCING   41

PROTECTIVE SHEATH   47

YES/NO RESPONSES (DOWSING)   48

COLORS and SOUND   50

INDIVIDUALS COLOR   50

MEDITATION   51

DIVINATION   59

MINERAL WATER - (GEM ELIXIR)   61

THE AURA   63

REINCARNATION   65

MEDIUMS   66

CHANNELLING   67

CRYSTAL & GEMSTONE THERAPY   68

HEALING.   69

USING THE DETAILED LIST OF CRYSTALS   72

CONTENTS - Con't

3. Details on Selected Crystals & Gems   74

4. Cross Reference for Gem Names   156

5. The Zodiac   163

6. Physical Ailments   169

7. Appendix   185

8. Index   187

Note that this book is designed as a long term reference book, and as such is being continually replaced by newer releases. To receive the updated version, send the update page at the rear to the address shown and updates will be forwarded as released. Your comments are most welcome.

Acknowledgements

My thanks go to Cesare, Debbie, Fiona, Gae, Jenny, Judi, Julie, Kim, Vicky, Wanders, and my personal spirit guides for variously encouraging me to keep going when I felt like giving up; for advising me when I was in danger of losing the plot; for putting a database package together so the book could be made available on disk; for proof reading and offering suggestions; for cover design; for typographical advice; for details on the zodiac; for increasing my understanding of minerals, and for just being there when I needed support. Without them, I would not have been able to complete the task. Thank You.

1. My Introduction to Crystals

LET'S SET THE SCENE.

Some facts to start with:

Firstly, crystals and gems have been used for healing by various "primitive" or "native" peoples for thousands of years.

Secondly, numerous records suggest that subsequent events led those people to believe that positive results followed as a direct consequence of using the crystals and gems.

We, as a different culture, having been brought up with different concepts and beliefs, may or may not give credence to the same cause-and-effect relationship. We could argue that it was the power of positive thinking or some other equally plausible alternative that produced the result, but that does not change the belief system of those peoples. They believed crystals and gems had special powers, and believed beneficial results were achieved by their use.

(Minerals is the correct definition for what we refer to as crystals and gemstones, although there are gems that are not minerals at all, as you will discover as you read on. In this book I am following the common usage of crystals for the quartz family and gemstones for the rest).

In the present day, females are variously credited with having a sixth sense or "the power of intuition". This is particularly true for those of the non Western world, Australian Aborigines, American Indians and the like, but it is also true of many females of our modern Western society. They are aware of what they "feel" and "sense", and whether or not the there is a direct relationship, they are also quite relaxed about believing in the power of crystals, and other "supernatural" phenomenon. Who, for example, reads and listens to the stars every day? Many of you will say that the men do, but largely it is the ladies who are the avid followers of horoscopes.

By contrast, their male partners have in general, closed their collective mind to the abnormal, and we may well ask whether it is because they have been taught to examine every claim and event analytically. If an event or claim cannot be substantiated by its ability to be replicated, then it is not "real". They have been taught that nothing can happen without concrete and observable criteria. The result, for whatever reason, is that the average male does not have the same acceptance of supernatural events as does his female counterpart.

However, it may be possible to influence the men of our time to open their minds to the benefits to be had from a greater understanding and acceptance of what I call "The Crystal Kingdom". Why I want to influence the male of the species about the importance of crystals will be answered in the next few pages.

Why are men not aware?

As one young lady in her mid twenties, said to me recently, "We cannot be here (on earth) just to earn money to live, experience life, procreate and then die. There MUST be more to it than that". She has obviously opened her mind to alternatives, and will happily consider them whenever they may come along. She could even be thought of as actively seeking alternatives. I can never remember a young man saying anything which indicated that he was even vaguely receptive to an alternative. When directly questioned however, men generally accept that there is something "out there" that they do not fully understand, although they do not display any great desire to explore it either, leaving that to Captain Kirk and the crew of his famous space ship, - "Enterprise".

The reasons for having a closed attitude to unscientific findings is arguably a phenomenon of the modern or Western culture. For the last several hundred years, the Western world has had decisions made by people in authority, including religious leaders, monarchs, scientists, dictators, military leaders etc., who believed that theirs was the only answer and would not tolerate any serious counter argument. They had no training or knowledge handed onto them, but for a variety of reasons found themselves "in charge" and did what they thought best at the time. When we move away from the "advanced" world we find quite a different story. Men from the third world, the American Indian, the Australian Aborigine, the Tribal African and so on, all have a much more open, accepting attitude to subjective knowledge than those in Western cultures. Their leaders are groomed for a position of authority with information being handed down from tribal elders with a large part of the rituals based on supernatural activities. It is therefore reasonable to deduce that what prevents males from having an inquiring and open mind about the supernatural, is not so much a matter of genetics, as the culture in which they have been conditioned.

The other side of the argument suggests we consider the possibility that human behaviour is inherited. This argument proposes that we inherit from our forebears genes predisposing us to the attitudes we later display. In other words, it is not only the physical body that is influenced by the genes received from our parents, but also information relating to our expectations, dreams, intuition, and the like. Going a little further, is it possible that karma is genetically imprinted within us at birth? I simply do not have enough knowledge to pass judgement, and I have an open mind on the subject. Putting aside for a moment the origins of the attitudes we hold in modern Western society, the indoctrination within our society perpetuates the myth of the unscientific and unsubstantiated. Although information on the supernatural is available, it is only found by those who go looking for it. And there is a degree of pressure not to look too hard.

An example is that of Edgar Cayce who was born in 1877 - over one hundred years ago. By the time he was twenty years old he was able to diagnose illness in people whom he had never met or seen. This he did in hypnotic trances. During most of his life time, he was criticised as a charlatan and con man, simply because the scientists of his time could not explain how he did what he did. He left over thirty thousand documented cases of his work, yet failed to earn the respect of, or recognition by the scientific community. That he was obtaining his medical information and results by some means other than conventional, resulted in continued investigations in the hope that his "tricks" would be revealed. Those who received help from Cayce and subsequently recovered from their illness, had tried conventional medicine first without benefit. It was of little concern to them whether it was conventional or alternative medicine that alleviated their problem. They just wanted to get better. Even now, at the end of the twentieth century, although information about alternative healing processes is readily available, it is found only by those who actively search for it. The more orthodox world applies pressure not to do so. One example is the refusal of many medical benefit funds to refund any part of alternative therapy expenses.

For those women and smaller number of men in the Western world who are in tune with the "other world", the conviction they hold may be the result of "receiving" advice telepathically, perhaps following the death of a loved one; possibly the result of a fortune telling which indicates an event that actually comes to pass, or maybe the association of someone who is apparently "guided" by some unknown spirit. It may have come about through a "deja vu" experience re-living an event - a feeling that we have all experienced at one time or another. Another possibility is dreams. Thousands upon thousands of dreams were analysed by Dr. David Ryback Ph. D., a professor of psychology who came to the conclusion that dreams in as many as half the population can be interpreted as advice about the FUTURE. In most cases the dreamer did not talk about these dreams until questioned because they believed people would think them strange, yet these "psychic" dreams are very vivid and require little interpretation. For those interested in the subject, the book is *Dreams That Come True* by Dr. David Ryback Ph. D.

The understanding that is accepted by these more "open" individuals includes something other than human life as we understand it. Rather than try to define exactly what it is that they believe, let us simply accept the fact that they believe there are "Gods", "The Force", "Spirits", "Guides", "Beings", or whatever we wish to call them, out there. Unfortunately, the vast majority of people do not open their minds to the same possibility, - that something greater than ourselves is available for us to contact. I believe all we have to do is to open ourselves to accept the communication.

Not so many years ago, the wrist radio of comic strip character Dick Tracy was a fantasy. In a very short period of time, we have come to the point where a portable phone is not much bigger than Dick Tracy's wrist radio, and can contact anyone in the whole world. Using this analogy, it is not so difficult to believe that there are communications being conducted using methods we do not yet understand, being received by receptive individuals. As one male who has for many years, closed off alternative thoughts and pathways, I hope to provide enough reasons to encourage you to least consider what it is going on around you, and invite you to open up to other forms of communication.

If you are female, you are possibly ahead of us mere males, so please bear with us for a little time, while we try to catch up. Females who have not become aware of, or not yet interested in these forces, may benefit from opening their minds to the same processes.

WHERE DO WE START?

Speaking personally I was brought up to believe that if the psychic world existed, and I was far from certain that it did, it could only do me harm if I ever "got involved". I never considered that the spiritual world had good spirits as well as the evil ones flashed onto movie screens in increasingly loathsome encounters. At this "evil" level, there was pagan worship, blood offerings on alters, raping of virgins, and so on.

At the other end of the spectrum, I was told that a belief in God and His Church was an absolute minimum to save my soul. That if I attended Bible readings, Masses, and other appropriate services, all would be well. My soul would go to heaven when I died, and I would be rewarded by being able to spend all the rest of my (dead) life with God and hopefully, my parents and relatives, all of which was very comforting to a small boy. From the very beginning, I was conditioned not to believe in spirits other than the ones the Church invented or approved of. My schooling reinforced this process with "proof" and "repeatability" required before one should believe in anything that was offered. The Church was somehow excused from this process, because it got there first, and laid down the rule that you could not change their rules.

This is not to say that I analysed everything offered to me. As with most teenagers, it depended on what alternative tasks awaited when school was over for the day. If the task was shopping with Mum, then I might be prepared to ask questions of the teacher so I could avoid the shopping chore, however if I thought I might have a chance to talk to my "heart throb" Laura on the way home, then in no way was I interested in pursuing the educational matter any further. As the years (and Laura) passed, I sometimes looked up at the stars on a clear night, marvelled at it all, and asked myself, "What is the purpose of this life?", or "Why am I here?" I never did receive an answer, largely because I did not know how to receive the answer, even if one came. The only way I could have received an answer to my question was for some Greater Being to have placed an advertisement in the personal column of the newspaper as follows:

"Attn: Bryan - Your purpose in this life is to grow up, join the Army, get married, start a career, have two children, get divorced, spend some time single, find another partner, realise that there is a good reason why you are here, work at that, and spend the rest of your life as happily as you can. Do not worry about anything else, we have it all under control". As I did not usually read the personal columns, however, I would have missed it anyway.

Like most of the people in the Western world, I went on doing what I did, ignoring anything that was mystical, seeing only what was very concrete and very obvious. I certainly did not bother to follow up the doubts that were at the back of my mind. If I thought about it at all, I did not believe I had the ability or methodology to resolve the sort of questions forming in my mind, so I continued my quiet life, being what I had been conditioned to be. It was easy to do nothing, and as long as one did not know about these matters, it was easy to disregard the doubts and questions.

MY FIRST STEP

I am sure it is different for everyone, but my first awakening was when I attended a course about hypnotism, a subject which had fascinated me for years. Here was an opportunity to find out more, and maybe even derive some benefit. To cut a long story short, there was no one more surprised than I, when I first hypnotised myself, and instructed my right arm to raise itself six inches off the arm-rest of the chair. After a short delay, it did, and I nearly dropped through the floor. My arm raised itself, by itself!!

I remember recounting the circumstances to a fellow course attendee, and he had experienced similar feelings. I just could not believe that something other than my arm muscles were moving my arm. It certainly was not me, (not consciously, anyway), and it did not get tired staying up for a long time. I went home, and over the next few months repeated the process, carrying on a "conversation" with my "unconscious" mind, which is what I was told was controlling the movement of my arm. I had finally come to believe that there was something called (for convenience at least), my unconscious (or subconscious) mind. I accepted for the first time, a "spirit" (in that I could not see it or touch it), other than the God I had learned about as a boy. I had taken the first step on my journey of discovery. In this case the first step was a relatively safe one, as it was still my unconscious mind, my arm, my hypnotism, and nobody else's. Long before I took the next step, I continued to ignore what was patently obvious to me, - that I really should look further into this whole subject. The reasons I did not follow up my initial feelings, I believe, were two fold; firstly, I wanted to be "normal" in the eyes of my peer group, and not to be seen to be involved in "fringe activities"; and secondly, I think I was afraid of what I might find out.

MY SECOND STEP

The second step was virtually thrust upon me. A period of about five years had passed since my "arm raising" awakening. During an interstate trip, my best friend introduced me to a lady who did "readings" of the aura surrounding each of us. The reading I was told, was much like Tarot card reading, except that this lady "interpreted" the condition of one's various bodies (emotional, physical, spiritual, etc), and messages they were trying to pass on. This was all new to me, but as I had nothing to lose, I arranged to meet with Grace.

We spent a couple of hours that first time. She told me I had a blockage in my heart chakra, of which I was not aware. In fact I was not even aware of chakras! She continued for twenty or thirty minutes, covering many and various points about events in my past lives. I was not entirely sure about this point, but did not dismiss it totally either. She asked me to be patient for a few minutes and closed her eyes, after which she told me she had been told that my purpose in this life was to work with crystals, and that the time was fast approaching when I should commit myself to this task. She said that I had attracted some very powerful spirit guides, which usually happened when one was a powerful person themselves. She was being told that I was such a person and this confirmed her earlier feelings. The remainder (and the majority) of the time was spent describing previous experiences I had had with crystals, about the spirit guides ("guardian angels" to me), who were accompanying me in this lifetime, the direction my life might conceivably take, and the like. The details of my past lives interested me greatly as many events in this life seemed to "fall into place" with this knowledge.

That meeting affected me greatly. The idea of having previous lives made some sense. My natural association with certain activities also seemed logical. I was not so sure about being spiritually powerful, but our ego is attracted to that sort of thing, and I was no exception. I decided it was pretty stupid to worry about what others might think or say. The significance of the matter was that I was being told I had a purpose in this life, and that it was up to me whether I chose to follow it in a more resolute way. My decision was to keep an open mind and as opportunities opened up, move toward the "spiritual" perspective.

I returned home on a Friday evening, and before retiring for the night, listened to the tape recording I had made of the reading. On the Saturday morning I went shopping very early. When I had finished the supermarket shopping, I took the most unlikely step of walking down the street to a "psychic" shop, despite the fact that I knew it would be closed at that early hour. In the window I read a small hand-written notice describing an introductory course in crystal healing. I took down the number, and rang it at the more respectable time of 9:30 or so, and left a message on the answering machine I encountered. A short time later the lady running the course returned the call, and advised that there was indeed one vacancy on the course starting the following Saturday. Finding it difficult to explain the coincidences (?) occurring, I enrolled to attend the course and so, took one more step on my journey.

Now that my interest was aroused, I found time to visit several bookshops, looking for books about crystals, and started to develop an understanding of the terminology used. Initially I did not even know which section of the shop to look for information about crystals, but eventually stumbled across it. I purchased a couple of books, introductory in their nature, and read them with a great deal of interest. I became more interested in my own crystals and gems, and realised that I had been unconsciously collecting them. I had an amethyst cluster, emeralds, tiger's eye, several clear quartz crystals, carnelian, pearls, sapphire, and some others I liked but could not identify. I had been given some and had purchased others at fairs or stalls because they "felt good". I had to come to terms with the fact that I had been "dabbling" in the world of crystals without being aware of it. I had been on the fringe, perhaps benefiting without even being conscious of it. Having accepted that, I started to question what gems I should use, and whether I should use the same gems for different things, but before I could answer that question, the day of the course arrived, and I headed off to learn about crystal healing.

The course covered basic information on healing using gems, their individual properties, their differences, why each was unique, how to clean gems and why it was necessary, the seriousness of the healing, and a real "live" healing carried out on one of the students.

The healing was carried out with the gemstones being selected by the healer based on her intuitive understanding of what was required. The gemstones were laid on the student in the area of the body where the healer felt they would be most appropriate, the other students being advised as to why they were used and why the specific area was chosen, as well as the likely or desired effects. The course leader chanted and called on spirit guides to assist with the healing, and burned incense. It was all very intense. I absorbed it all with a great deal of interest but found it difficult to integrate the activities with my understanding of the healing process. Knowing that it was a lot to absorb in a short time, I was relaxed about letting it slowly filter into my conscious understanding. I enrolled in a follow-up course to be held about a month later, which was to be conducted over three days. I felt it likely that by then I would have processed the knowledge gathered at the earlier course and be ready for more.

During the month between courses, I read more on the subject and listened twice to the tape from the previous reading. For reasons I did not understand, I decided that the next course was not for me. My feelings were telling me that this method of healing was not compatible with my instinctive knowledge, and that I should cancel my enrolment. So instead of attending the course, I went about researching the topic by more reading. It was to be more than a year before my decision to cancel that course proved to be sound. This is in no way to suggest that the healing process I observed was not correct, simply that it was not consistent with my intuitive understanding.

MY THIRD STEP

Just as my first two steps (the hypnotism and reading) came into my life in unusual circumstances, the third was no different. A very good friend who knew of my interest suggested I should speak to a lady who "channels". I was not quite sure what I was getting into, but arranged to meet Gae. To my surprise, channelling never entered the conversation. Gae is one of those people who knows so much that it made me realise how much I have yet to learn. We discussed my reading (my second step), which I believe is the real start of my present journey, and she helped to clarify some of the areas about which I was still confused. Gae commented that I was putting out a huge amount of energy, and asked if I was aware of it, which I was not. In the next half hour or so, she confirmed that she could "see" me working as a crystal master in past lives. I was also moving in the same direction in a strong way in this life. I found it very refreshing that I could talk about previous lifetimes, past events and the like, without being made to feel that I had taken leave of my senses.

Gae confirmed the earlier reading that crystals was where my immediate future lay, and I should follow it in whatever manner seemed appropriate, doing whatever felt right to me. The strong energy that was evident to her apparently meant that I was coming into my time and I should "go with the flow". This I did, visiting her several more times as she was one of the few people with whom I could be completely open. During one visit she mentioned a spiritual teacher who was coming to Australia from the USA, who ran courses in meditation and self-awareness. It seemed appropriate that I should attend one of his courses.

MY FOURTH STEP

The course changed my life. Firstly I attended the open nights and was impressed, but sceptical. I decided to attend the weekend (Friday evening, Saturday, Sunday), "empowerment" program which *is designed to create a unique transformational environment in which everyone is assisted to move beyond their current limitations into a truer perception of the transcendental nature of reality. What unfolds is a totally new range of experience which is subtle, powerful and expansive,* (their words).

I would describe the weekend as one in which I was "blown away". The group had the deepest meditation session and increased energy build up in each person I have ever experienced. There was just so much energy around us, and in us, it is impossible to express or describe it adequately. The changes that it brought up in me will continue to become apparent for a long time to come. Whilst deep in meditation I confirmed to myself that I was on a journey, with crystal healing being the first step. Whatever happens after this I just do not know, but I know it will be proper for me.

It would be erroneous of me not to mention one more point about the weekend. I came home on the Sunday evening, with my head "pulsing", my body full of lovely feelings. I was on a "high", as if I was on drugs or whatever, but it was all being created inside my head. I had been opened up from the inside and I liked what was happening. I sensed that I was a little "down", and attributed the melancholy to the fact that the weekend empowerment was over. In a subsequent meditation that evening on my own, the real reason for my uneasiness became apparent. I was scared. Scared of what I was undertaking, scared of leaving all that I knew as safe and comfortable for the unknown, the untried, the unexplained. I had been opened up, and realised for the first time just how serious the implications of my decision to follow my feelings might be.

That night and the following day I found myself depressed and unhappy to the point of crying. I cannot remember the previous time I had cried. Fortunately for me, being a product of Western upbringing, there was nobody to see the release of my emotions. I was afraid, and it was showing. I could not remember ever being afraid like this before. A quick call to Gae to confide in her gave me reassurance, although she did confirm that during the weekend she had been worried about me as I had obviously been dragging up information from the inner depths of my mind and she was not sure how I had been processing it. As she said, "Your journey is awesome, and I do not know if you fully understand the immensity of it, even now. Maybe your unconscious mind knows, and you are getting a glimpse of it and that is what is scaring you". The end result was that I felt both uplifted and a little more afraid. Gae had become one of my teachers. She is assisting me on my journey, and has become a special friend.

At the weekend empowerment program, we had been told to make sure we came to the early Tuesday evening session, to release the excess energy that was within us. Just as I was amazed at the build-up of the energy on the Friday evening, I was equally amazed how, during the one hour "stretch and release" session, it was all dissipated. I felt like I was back to normal, but had experienced something special. That episode being over, I returned to my more mundane life. As I have already said, I am not sure of the direction of my future, and I am a bit scared, but I only have myself to be scared of. I know if I really have to, I can stop and regroup at any time. I also know that I want to undertake this journey, as it is what I am on this planet to do.

MY DIRECTION CLARIFIED

Gae introduced me to another lady who does Tarot reading and Astrology. Judi did a tarot reading for me and confirmed the direction and pace at which I was going. The tarot reading was special in many ways, not the least of which was the huge amount of energy that surrounded the two of us during the reading, which indicated that I had some definite competence in some areas, and that my chosen direction was right for the powers that I possessed.

I found it more difficult to ignore information coming from three "external" sources and my own meditation telling me my future was involved with crystals in some way. Although feeling afraid, I felt I now had my future more clearly defined than ever before, and felt much more confident about moving ahead. By this time "thoughts" were popping into my head quite randomly, without me having any idea of where they were coming from. These ranged from the names of people who were not known to me with whom I should make contact, to details on minerals and how they could be used in healing, to words which turned out to be terms used in new age healing. At this time I decided to start recording on a personal tape recorder anything that I did not understand so that I could hold it for future reference without having to categorise it and physically file it away.

One of the first directives received in this manner was to put to use all the information I had gathered about crystals and healing for a much wider audience. By this time I had read about forty different books on the subject, and could understand other people's difficulty in assimilating the information. My immediate task therefore, was to present the information in a more manageable form. Although it did not seem to support my previous involvement with crystal healing, I decided that I should follow my feelings and develop this book as I felt I was being guided.

One problem I encountered as I read the various books, was that I found myself being frustrated at my rate of progress. What became obvious to me as a long-time computer user, used to looking up a menu and going straight to the item required, was that I had to read most books from beginning to end to get the context right. I could not find a book which was organised so that I could turn to information about specific areas, such as gemstones for a given birthday, the beneficial effects claimed or how to use a given gemstone, any cautionary notes, associated stones, colors involved, charkas affected, and the like.

I wanted to have it all catalogued, so that I would be able to move from topic to topic, locate the information required and any pointers to related information, and so on. All of this can be achieved by good indexing methods into a computer database, so I decided that as well as a written document, I would make the information available in computer form for those who would find it more acceptable. I felt that if I could make it easy for you to associate gemstones, effects, medical ailments, colors, chakras, anniversaries, the zodiac, and so on, all on your personal computer, I may save you some time and effort, as well as increasing your knowledge of crystals. "Context sensitive information" (a computer term) ensures you can acquire your knowledge in the shortest possible time.

One thing I learnt from the computer industry is that manuals date very quickly. To overcome this, most software products offer an update service, which includes a new book and a disk with the latest information on it, and I feel this procedure is appropriate for this venture. As my knowledge of crystals and healing increases, I can make it available to both readers and computer users alike. I have no doubt that I will move into many other areas which may be of interest to some readers and information about these areas will be included. The updated book and disk will available at minimal cost, so that the initial investment you have made will continue to be of value.

For those people who do not yet have enough interest in crystals to purchase the book or disk, I will make available specific topics in the form of "templates", a laminated sheet, A4 in size. (A4 is the standard letter size). The lamination will prevent the sheets being lost, soiled or damaged. I feel confident that these templates will be available to a wider audience than the book itself due in part to their negligible cost, and it satisfies my desire to distribute the details I have accumulated to a wider cross section of the community.

Studying crystals lead me to all sorts of related areas, including such things as affirmations, aroma therapy, astrology, chakras, channelling, clairvoyance, color healing, divination, dowsing, energy centres, healing, iridology, karma, kundalini, meditation, re-incarnation, somnambulism, tarot reading, the new age, past life therapy, psychic awareness, vibrational healing, and many more. As I tried to absorb what each meant and where it fitted, I found many apparent contradictions and have not yet satisfied myself as to the significance of some. Those that I understand are in this release, and the others will appear in future releases of the book and disk.

HOW I ARRIVED TO THIS POINT

It is worth outlining a little of my background in order to understand why this journey of discovery is very significant to me. After leaving school, I migrated to Australia with my older brother, leaving our family in Scotland. Once in Australia, I joined the Australian Army and after training was sent to Malaya (now Malaysia), returned to Australia and to civilian life and went to work for a variety of companies, always studying to improve myself. I changed jobs several times, receiving promotion and salary increases with each move. Like most others of my generation, I married, and had two lovely children who are now grown up. Like many others, I had the urge to leave paid employment and establish my own business.

In my case, I set up a consulting business for computers which were then in their infancy. When my children were in their mid teens my wife and I separated, which had become the prevalent thing to do in those days. I became a so-called success, and had an enduring business relationship with my co-owner and partner. We owned and operated one of the more successful computer software companies, which employed over fifty people, with offices in all states and several overseas countries. Recognised as one of the leaders in the computer software industry, the Company was a finalist in the Small Business Awards, won the first Australian Design Award for software, and as the pinnacle of my success, I received the industry recognised "Achiever of the Year" award. Although it may appear that these accomplishments are not directly related to crystal awareness, having achieved a great deal by "normal" standards, it caused me to examine carefully my reasons for setting out on this journey into the unknown.

As you are probably aware, the left side of the brain controls the right side of the body and is used for the more logical or deductive type reasoning, whereas the right side of the brain controls the left side of the body and the "feeling" or intuitive decisions we make. By virtue of the achievements I had attained in business, the left side of my brain appeared to be working quite well for me. In order that I can start to understand the new world I am moving into, I now have to develop the right side of my brain. Unlike my approach in the business world, my new journey does not now have a "master plan", with budgets, goals and targets. I do not know where I am going, how I am going to get there or even how I know IF I have arrived there. You may well understand why I am a little scared. I am giving up a perfectly respectable, reasonably comfortable, fully controlled life, for something totally unknown. I simply do not know where this journey will take me. Whilst I am a little scared, I am also optimistic, and up to this point, I have had some fantastic luck - if it really is luck, and have become involved with many wonderful people.

Whether I continue to develop in the area of crystal healing or move onto some other area, I do not know, but I believe I came here with a specific purpose and plan, and am prepared to go through with it. So far, I have become relatively skilled at using crystals in a healing way, although I often feel that I have not achieved as much as I would have liked. Feedback from my clients indicates they undergo changes with which they are satisfied so I have to learn to accept that something appropriate has been achieved, and by increasing my awareness I will become even more skilled at helping others to resolve their problems. I must stress however, that I do not believe I am a healer in the purest sense. Healing may take place when I assist clients by to utilise their unused resources, but it is they who are healing themselves. The crystals provide energy, and I am merely an agent through which the crystals work to help the client.

WHERE TO NOW?

The reader may speculate as to why have I told the above story. Simply, there may be many people like myself, who could begin to consciously and deliberately consider what they are doing with their lives. By doing so, they may find a whole new world that is vaguely familiar and attractive to them. Many individuals will consider it inappropriate to change their current life-style because of other priorities, or may be unable to see that there is a way in which they can change. For many others not bound by such personal circumstances, it will simply be a matter of being honest with themselves, recognising that they, like me, have a calling, whether they particularly like it or not.

For those individuals, it is likely they will recognise that investigation is at least warranted, and by simply opening themselves to receive the information surrounding them, the journey can begin. This does not mean that they are expected to throw away all their hard-earned assets and join a bunch of wandering gipsies. Within each individual's frame of reference, understanding, talents and ability to contribute, a way will be revealed that is compatible and acceptable to them. It may be that some become healers; others may have skills at oratory or lecturing which can be used to increase the awareness of the population at large; others again may have a business or trade union background that can help influence the direction of a project; many more may be parents who will allow their children to grow up understanding the presence of auras; and for others it may be encouraging their friends to an understanding of the higher self. Lots of individuals have a part to play, all in a manner that is consistent and congruent with their particular life style. No one is being asked to throw away anything. What everyone is being asked to do is simply to expand their horizons.

Rather than examining what it is that we might have to sacrifice in taking up this challenge, perhaps we should remember the question raised by the young lady to whom I referred earlier in this book, "we cannot be here (on earth) just to earn money to live, experience life, procreate and then die. There MUST be more to it than that". Perhaps we who are challenged, are the lucky ones. On an individual basis each of us must decide whether to pursue the matter further, or let the opportunity lapse. Both are valid options, and the decision made should be after serious consideration. If you decide you should go further, you will find that there are many alternatives and paths. By reading this and other books, you may then be in a more informed position to select an area that seems to appeal to you. Follow your feelings and explore whatever comes your way, allowing yourself to be open and accepting. You will almost certainly have to backtrack at some points, but that is how we learn. We are often more aware of what is not right for us than what is right for us.

On a personal basis, I am continuing to provide computer consulting, but am cutting it back to an average of two - three days per week. I earn enough from those activities to permit me to live in an acceptable manner, whilst providing me time to develop my awareness of crystals. I know I have many years of learning ahead of me, and can only take one step at a time. I believe my journey is a long one, and despite the fact that I sometimes think I am going too slowly, I marvel at just how far I have come in only a few years. If I had sufficient resources, I would devote myself entirely to crystals and healing, but as I do not, I will continue my own process of development, some crystal healing and development of this book and disk. With a group of like-minded people, an appropriate location is being sought to establish a healing centre, so that a larger number of clients can be assisted.

The remainder of this book (and disk) represent the distillation of data that I have assembled. I wish I could tell you where it came from, but all I know is that I start typing and words and phrases pop into my head. When I review the information, I find a substantial part of it agrees with other authorities on the subject. Where I differ, I can only suggest that I have been told to write it this way.

I am moving ahead on my personal journey, are you coming?

Love is the key - we are all supplied

with a blank and make of it what we

choose

2. Some Background Information On:

CRYSTAL & MINERALS - DEFINITIONS

The term "crystals" usually refers to members of the Quartz family. This includes Amethyst, Citrine, Clear (or Rock) Quartz, Rose Quartz, Smoky Quartz, and Strawberry and Blue Quartz, unusual and uncommon varieties. For the purposes of this book, "gemstones" refer to all other minerals, including some non-minerals such as Amber, which is the sap of trees. As there are more than 3,000 minerals, it would be impracticable to include them all in this book, so only the more significant from a healing point of view, more popular or more readily available have been researched. The list will be expanded and developed in future releases of this book and disk. Diamond, Sapphire and Ruby are included, although they are more properly called precious stones because of their relative scarcity and greater monetary value.

Imitations of gemstones are common and can deceive all but the experienced practitioner. You should therefore acquaint yourself with the non genuine articles as early as you can, as they do not possess the same healing qualities. A typical example is treating some common quartz crystals with microwave radiation (in a microwave oven), where they change color, appearing to be something they are not. Although the crystal has been "impaired", it can be healed by a crystal practitioner.

HISTORY OF CRYSTALS

If you are already familiar with crystals, you may wish to pass on to the next section, as the following is a "thumb nail sketch" background to crystals. The word "crystals" in this section refers only to quartz crystals, not other minerals.

Crystals were used in the ancient civilisations of Lemuria and Atlantis, of which we usually only associate with the lost city of..... It is believed the people who inhabited Atlantis used crystals in ways that are not yet fully understood by us for communication, as power sources, in transportation, and in all sorts of healing. Information has been gathered by psychics who have told us that there were certain people on Atlantis who were misusing crystals for their own selfish means. In the time of Atlantis, unlike Wall Street, this was a big "No-No", and resulted in the legendary catastrophe.

There was however, sufficient time for warnings of the imminent destruction to be passed to powerful individuals who programmed information into crystals and scattered them around the planet to lie dormant until a new generation was ready to use the information. Some of those crystals (called teacher, transmitter and channelling crystals) have already surfaced in various parts of the world, but it is understood that there are many, many more to be discovered. These will appear when it is proper for them to do so. These special crystals have specific tasks such as the passing on of information, enhancing psychic powers and telepathic communications. Other ancient civilisations that used crystals (including a number of gemstones as well as quartz crystals), in a variety of ways were the Incas, the Egyptians, and the Aztecs. Again, like Atlantean's, healing was one of the main benefits for which crystals and gems were used. This healing included emotional, as well as physical healing, and assisted in spiritual development of individuals.

Unfortunately for us, most of the information on the use of crystals was lost along the way, leading to the development of conventional medicine and healing that exists today. Currently however, crystal healing is experiencing a resurgence, a new wave of popularity, as more and more people realise that many ailments in the body can be healed without resorting to chemicals. (This is not to suggest that crystals should replace modern medicine, simply live alongside it). It appears that more of the previously skilled practitioners who lived on Atlantis and Leumaria are now returning to the planet, and although they return with the knowledge previously gathered, many of them are not aware of it. They go through life unaware of their special abilities, until some event triggers an awakening in them. It may be that when they are holding a crystal for example, they "feel" or "receive" information. This is usually ignored, dismissed as coincidence, or raises fear and misunderstanding in the individual. Bearing in mind the pressure to be conventional by ones' peer group discussed earlier, it is not surprising that uncertainty prevails.

As time passes, more and more of these individuals who would otherwise be considered perfectly rational human beings, are facing their fear and accepting that they have an unusual skill. They are here to re-establish crystals to their rightful place in healing, and are getting on with the job. As this new age of crystals continues to unfold, many more people are taking part in the process. Although this book is concerned principally with crystals, it is appropriate to remind the reader that conventional medicine is also seeking remedies from rain forests and other areas of nature, that there is an upsurge in homoeopathy, naturopathy, other natural medicines, acupuncture, acupressure, and so on. The number of people successfully treating cancer without drugs increases every day. This indicates that there is greater acceptance of healing by means other than the conventional, including healing with crystals.

To highlight the power of crystals, if any is needed, I will recount a story involving a lady I know. She borrowed a crystal cluster of mine, at my suggestion, as she seemed to be "in tune" with it. She took it home and gave it pride of place on her breakfast bar,

Crystals: The Journey Begins - Are You Coming?

where, to use her words, "It brightened up the whole room". A few weeks later when I was to pick it up, she commented that although it looked great, it did not really "do" anything. My response was "Well, that's fine, it may not be appropriate yet", not being sure what it should have "done". The lady did however mention in passing that she had more energy than normal over the last few weeks and had achieved a great deal around the house and garden. It would have been hard for me to convince her that there was any connection, so I did not even try, and in fact, I had no basis to suggest that the crystal cluster was responsible for her higher energy level.

As I was leaving, we discussed her garden, which is a real picture. She had one plant that was trying to reach the sun, stretching itself from a low shrub to a slender tree to squeeze between the house and a very large tree. I remarked that I had recently heard of a lady who had a plant on her kitchen bench where the leaves grew AWAY from the window and towards a crystal that had been in the room. Her expression made me think I had just arrived from Mars or somewhere equally unlikely. "Come in and look at this" she said and led me back into the house. There on the breakfast bar was a Monsteria Deliciosa plant, about three feet high, growing AWAY from the window to where the crystal had been. "That has been doing that over the last week or so, and I could not work it out. So much so, that I have had to tie it up to stop it falling over again".

The change of direction of the plant's growth was so marked that she had been discussing it with her daughter, and neither of them could work out why this plant should suddenly start to grow away from the light source that it had always grown towards. The leaves started to grow so directly toward the crystal that, as it bent over, the whole arrangement (plant, container etc), over-balanced and fell, requiring it to have a string attached to secure it firmly to the window frame. Within a week of the removal of the crystal, the plant was back at its original position, trying to get out through the window. I would have been inclined to say the story had been exaggerated had I had not seen it for myself, but it confirmed for me the powerful energy that a quartz cluster has. I have mentioned this example rather than many others involving people, as it is easy for us to seek alternatives to justify the results.

An interesting experiment can be carried out simply by purchasing two bunches of flowers. Fill one vase with the second flower of each bunch, with the remainder being placed into a second vase. Into one vase put a clear quartz crystal, either single or cluster and fill both vases with water from the same source, and wait for a few days. You will soon see that "something" is going on. The vase with the crystal will have healthy flowers for longer than the other, despite the fact that both bunches were intermixed prior to placing them in the vases. Try it - you will be surprised at the difference.

MASTER HEALERS

As discussed previously, the term "crystals" includes seven different color groups of which I believe clear quartz is the most important, and can be considered as a MASTER HEALER. Whether single or double terminated, cluster, twin or single, these master healers are capable of healing in a special way. They can heal any ailment or condition that any other gemstone can, and can be programmed for any valid purpose. (Clear Quartz can be completely clear, completely cloudy, or a mixture of clear and cloudy). They can be used on any chakra, and one principally clear and one principally cloudy work very effectively together. Clear quartz is generally regarded as having male characteristics, (positive polarity, pro-active), cloudy quartz has female characteristics, (negative polarity, receptive). In crystals where both clear and cloudy zones exist, the one with larger percentage is dominant, but activity is moderated by the contrasting force.

The simplest healing of all using clear quartz is obtained by lying on the floor and placing a single terminated male crystal at the top of the head and a similar female at the feet, with both pointing towards the body. This activates the energy field within the body. A distance of about 6 inches is suitable, and by remaining in position between the two crystals for about twenty minutes, healing will take place. Next in order of complexity is achieved by adding a crystal in the region of the heart chakra, preferably a male pointing towards the head, which accentuates the energy flow in the centre of the body. To increase the energy still further place a male on your right side near your hand pointing downwards, and a female on your left side pointing upwards. The object of any particular configuration is to concentrate the energy, and let the power of the crystals find the organs that need repair. Before attempting any healing, either for yourself or a client, it is advisable to send your love to the crystal, and ask the power of the crystal to assist your healing in the most appropriate way. Various arrangements of crystals and gems around the body can focus the energy of crystals to a specific area or organ within the body. A detailed analysis by a skilled practitioner of many years using more complicated layouts is to be found in the book *Love Is In The Earth - Laying-On-Of-Stones* by Melody. Naturally it is advisable to make sure that all crystals used are "clean" as described in the section on selecting and cleansing crystals and gemstones, below.

Minerals other than clear quartz provide a wealth of color, shape and texture not available in the quartz family, assisting practitioners and users alike to associate the color of a gem with its appropriate chakra. The emerald, for example, being green in color is associated with the heart chakra, as that is the part of body associated with the color green. In like manner, a red ruby would more naturally fit in with the base chakra. Chapter 2, Chakra Points and Balancing, details colors, gemstones and chakras. Skilled practitioners as well as novices will continue to use other gems as well as crystals as there are definite links between specific conditions and specific gems, although clear quartz is the only true MASTER HEALER.

GETTING YOUR OWN CRYSTAL/GEMSTONE

The important point to make here is that the selected crystal must "feel" or "look" right to you, depending on whether you predominantly use your feeling or visual faculties. If it does not, do not buy it. This may take a little practice since you may only have a vague idea of what you want when looking to acquire a crystal. In order to "feel" the vibrations being produced, most shop staff will not mind you holding a crystal in your hand whilst you look around the shop, or alternatively placing your hand above a crystal to sense any energy being given off. This is often detected by a "tingling" sensation on your skin above the point of the crystal. The other method of choosing a crystal is to look at a group of crystals, close your eyes, concentrate and ask for guidance in selecting an appropriate one. Open your eyes and see if any one crystal stands out. It may be that one is shining more brightly than the others, it may be that it is the smallest (or largest) in a group, and stands out for that reason. It may be that one seems "lonely" or perhaps "asks" you to select it. If one appeals, select it, and if none appeal, continue looking. If you decide not to buy, the staff of the shop will understand. Do not buy until the right crystal is found. Whatever crystal or gem is finally selected, it is necessary that it is cleansed before use.

CRYSTALS AND GEMS - CLEANSING METHODS

There are six methods of cleansing crystals and gemstones, collectively called gems in this instance. First of all however, it is important to understand why it is necessary to clean them at all.

If you are going to wear or have a gem close to you, you do not want to be affected by any of the negative energy that may be held by the gem. Even more care is needed if you are going to use gems to heal others. In this case, it is most important to remove any negativity that the gem may have absorbed during healing sessions. It is wise therefore to clean all gems used for healing before reusing. Remember that gems hold positive as well negative energy. If you feel depressed or "down", the gem you are handling or wearing can absorb some of this negativity. This is a normal part of everyday life. However, you should not leave this negative energy in the gem, but rather cleanse it whenever you feel better, asking that only the negative energy depart, leaving you with the accumulated positive energy you have been building up. You should initially cleanse all your gems thoroughly, see salt bath method, and thereafter, routinely cleanse once a month.

1. Salt Bath.

A container, preferably made of natural material such as crockery or clay, is partly filled with sea water at room temperature or tepid tap water, and if you have a filter to remove the poisons such as chlorine or fluoride from the tap water, so much the better. If using tap water, add one teaspoon of rock salts per cup of water. Rock salts are available from most health stores and some supermarkets. The gems should be totally submerged and be left for up to twenty four hours, after which they should be drained and dried using a soft cloth. For the first cleansing, and for thorough cleansing, put your gems outside in your garden to experience the effects of the elements (sun, rain, moon, etc). They should be left outside for at least twenty four hours but preferably longer, and up to a week is desirable if the moon is not large, (first quarter, last quarter). If you do not have a garden, use a pot plant on your balcony or window ledge, making sure it is secure. The important thing is to have the gems exposed to nature in a sensitive manner. On a regular basis, approximately monthly, re-cleanse all your gems even if you have not used them. For simple cleansing, half an hour in the water is adequate and it is not necessary to put your gems outside. It is not advisable to re-use the salt water for other gems.

2. Under Running Water.

Hold your gems under tepid water, remembering that water which is too hot or too cold can cause damage to the gems. If you are lucky enough to have access to the ocean or a stream, it is better to use that. Hold each gem for a period of several minutes, projecting positive thoughts to the universe, and ask that all negative energy contained in the gem be removed and dispersed. Ask for only positive energy that can do you good to remain in the gem. If you are sincere with your thoughts, you will succeed in removing any negative energy that can do you harm. After the cleansing, dry the gem with care using a natural cloth material, such as cotton or wool. You can now start to use your stone and have it hold positive thoughts for your good.

Cautionary note: Do not leave gems that can be affected by either water or rain in a position where they will get wet or you may damage your stone. See chapter 3 - "Details on selected crystals & gems" for information, or ask your supplier for advice.

3. Cluster Cleansing.

A cluster of either clear quartz or amethyst provides a very good and easy method of cleansing other gems. The cluster itself should be cleansed using the salt bath method described before placing the gem to be cleansed on the cluster for at least twenty four hours, but longer (two or three days) is better. You can use the cluster as the de facto home of your gem when it is not with you. Amethyst is generally thought of as being suitable for cleansing, whereas clear quartz is ideal for transferring its healing properties into your selected gem. It is useful to remember to clean your clusters at least once a month.

4. Incense.

Cedar, sage, or sandalwood sticks are burnt and the gems are bathed by surrounding them in the smoke. During this time, you should ask, as with the running water method, that all negative energy be removed. You can use incense sticks as a less expensive alternative.

5. Burying.

Burying your gems in the ground and leaving them there for a period of from two or three days to several weeks will cleanse them. You will have to be aware of the energy being given off to be sure that they are fully cleansed before you unearth them. Make sure you do not forget where you buried them, and remove the soil from around your gems in an appropriate manner. It is best to have gems that have points placed so they are pointing downwards. It is claimed that gems holding a lot of negative energy bury themselves deep into the ground, so be prepared to unearth them deeper than you buried them

6. Pyramid.

If you have access to a pyramid, you can place your gems under the pyramid for a period of at least 24 hours, but preferably two or three days. You should also consciously ask for the cleansing to take place.

GENERAL.

It is a good idea not to restrict yourself to only one method, so try some of the others, especially if you believe that one method is not fully cleansing a particular gem. Remember that you do not know the full history of the gems that come into your possession, and it is important that they do not transfer any negative energy to you. Whatever methods you use, (and it may be that you use them all at various times), be gentle, have positive thoughts whilst doing the work, request that only positive energy remain, and be sincere. In this way, the gems will be thoroughly cleansed and ready to serve you.

PROGRAMMING CRYSTALS

Crystals can be programmed to become holders of your personal data bank. They can also be transmitters, teachers, guides, meditators, and so on. There are several methods of programming crystals, ranging from rubbing one face of the crystal (from "blunt" end to pointy end), whilst mentally visualising the desired outcome. It will normally be necessary to continue the process for several minutes. When you feel that the crystal understands your request, you can stop. Remember, you should always start with a clean crystal and before asking the crystal to do something for you, send it all the love you have and ask it to use it in whatever way it determines most useful. Another method is to hold the crystal and meditate, asking that the programming is transferred to the crystal, again with all your love. (Crystals react to love, so give it unstintingly and you will have it returned one hundred fold). When you feel you have accomplished your task, the crystal is ready for use.

If you are preparing a dowsing crystal, hold the chain in your hand, concentrate, send it your love, and tell the crystal you want it to move in a clockwise direction. This may take a few minutes, and you may even have to "help" the crystal understand clockwise by assisting with the movement. However, once the crystal understands what you mean, it will obediently turn as directed. It is necessary to do the same for counter clockwise movement. You will then have a crystal that will turn in the desired direction when placed over the chakras, or for Yes/No answers.

CHAKRA POINTS & BALANCING

There are seven main chakras points or energy centres in our bodies. In addition we also have minor chakras in the palms of our hands, our ankles, our feet and at other locations. The main chakra points each have an associated color, which largely conform to the colors of the rainbow, (Red, Orange, Yellow, Green, Blue, Indigo, Violet). The association starts at the lower part of the body, the lowest energy centre, up through the torso until you reach the crown of the head. See the detailed list below. These seven energy centres are some of the points that link the various bodies which make up the aura described in chapter two. Each energy centre is associated with specific organs of the body, specific colors, and specific vibratory rates or sounds.

Energy centres should be "in balance", meaning that there should be no blockages typically caused by emotional disturbances. The removal of these blockages will allow energy to move freely, up and down, in and out, of all the energy centres, providing the whole body with the life-giving force needed for a peaceful, harmonious life, free of dis-ease. (Literally, ill at ease, out of order, out of step).

Whenever you react negatively to a situation such as a marriage break-up, or the unfair promotion of someone at work, or where someone has angered you, you will close one or more of your energy centres, either totally or partially. You will not be aware of it, as it happens subtly and unconsciously. As the negative emotion subsides with the passage of time, often many years later, the energy centre will remain closed, since it cannot magically open up by itself. The sooner this is rectified and the energy centre brought back into balance, the better for both the physical and the spiritual well-being of the body. Physical illness or dis-ease is often caused by emotional trauma, with specific illnesses caused by specific energy centres being closed off.

Crystals are one of the most effective methods by which energy centres can be opened, bringing the body back into balance.

Initially, I would encourage you to seek out an appropriate crystal healer who will be able to open up your energy centres, and bring you into a better state of balance. A few visits may be necessary to ensure that all centres are in balance and functioning correctly. When this happens, a feeling of peace and harmony will be experienced as never before. Once you have experienced a crystal healer balancing your chakras, you will be able to do it yourself with no difficulty.

Chakra balancing is achieved by placing a crystal suspended from a chain over the chakra points, one at a time, starting with the crown and moving down the body. By holding the crystal over the chakra point, the energy of the crystal and the energy of the chakra will interact, causing the crystal to move, in much the same way as two magnets can force each other to move. The chakras are the principal point of connection of several of our bodies, and it may be necessary to move the crystal up or down to establish which body is affecting the crystal the most. (For additional details on our different bodies, see the section headed "The Aura" later in this chapter). The movement of the crystal is usually circular (in either direction), but occasionally is more of a straight line. Allow the crystal to move for as long as necessary, and only remove it when it has slowed down to almost stopping. The velocity of the crystal can vary greatly from very slow gentle movements, to very fast, very wide movements with neither having greater significance.

The brow chakra is the next to be balanced, and the process described above is repeated for this chakra, followed by the remaining five chakras. It is more convenient if the client lies down for all but the first chakra, when sitting in a chair is most convenient. When all chakras have been balanced, it is important that a "protective sheath" be wrapped around the client, see details below. During chakra balancing, the client will normally experience a variety of sensations, including a tingling feeling, psychedelic images, and a dry throat.

Several crystal practitioners for whom I have a high degree of respect suggest that balancing of chakras should be carried out using specific clockwise and counter clockwise movements of the crystal. The suggested order has the crystal rotating clockwise at the crown for a male, with the direction of rotation changing at each chakra. Females have the crystal turning in the opposite direction and start with a counter clockwise movement at the crown. It may be appropriate for you to try this method, and if you wish to do so, it will be necessary for you to have a pre-programmed crystal to turn in the direction you require. You may be interested in the process discussed at some length in *Crystal Healing* by Edmund Harold, and *Love Is In The Earth - Laying-On-Of-Stones* by Melody. (Edmund's book was previously published under another name, but look for it under the title above. And Melody has two books with the same starting words, so look for ...Laying-On-Of-Stones).

Chakra Points And Relevant Details:

Chakra Name: Crown.
Location: Top of the head.
Chakra #: 7.
Color: Violet or White.
Gemstone: Amethyst or Herkimer Diamond.
Affects: Spiritual Alignment; Understanding of Creation.
Gland: Pineal or Pituitary.
Balance Direction for Males: Clockwise.
Balance Direction for Females: Counter Clockwise.

Chakra Name: Brow, (or third eye).
Location: Middle of forehead between eyebrows.
Chakra #: 6.
Color: Indigo.
Gemstone: Indicolite.
Affects: Psychic Abilities; Intuition.
Gland: Pituitary or Pineal.
Balance Direction for Males: Counter Clockwise.
Balance Direction for Females: Clockwise.

Chakra Name: Throat or neck.
Location: Centre of the throat.
Chakra #: 5.
Color: Blue.
Gemstone: Turquoise.
Affects: Communication; Spiritual.
Gland: Thyroid & Parathyroid.
Balance Direction for Males: Clockwise.
Balance Direction for Females: Counter Clockwise.

Chakra Points And Relevant Details:

Chakra Name: Heart.
Location: Centre of body, in line with heart.
Chakra #: 4.
Color: Green.
Gemstone: Aventurine or rose quartz.
Affects: Love; Emotions.
Gland: Thymus.
Balance Direction for Males: Counter Clockwise.
Balance Direction for Females: Clockwise.

Chakra Name: Solar Plexus.
Location: Base of Ribs.
Chakra #: 3.
Color: Yellow.
Gemstone: Citrine.
Affects: Will Power; Mind; Energy.
Gland: Pancreas.
Balance Direction for Males: Clockwise.
Balance Direction for Females: Counter Clockwise.

Chakra Name: Spleen.
Location: Vicinity of Navel.
Chakra #: 2.
Color: Orange.
Gemstone: Carnelian.
Affects: Desire.
Gland: Adrenal or Suprarenal.
Balance Direction for Males: Counter Clockwise.
Balance Direction for Females: Clockwise.

Chakra Points And Relevant Details:

Chakra Name: Root or base.
Location: Over the base of the spine.
Chakra #: 1.
Color: Red/Black.
Gemstone: Red Garnet.
Affects: Survival.
Gland: Gonads/Ovaries.
Balance Direction for Males: Clockwise.
Balance Direction for Females: Counter Clockwise.

Each of the chakras resonate to a different sound. The sounds associated with each of the chakras alter with the passage of time and the personal development of each individual. Although I was initially led to believe that for the general population, the crown resonated to the sound of A, through to the base resonating to the sound of G, I am now not so sure. To be certain, you need access to tuning forks, and then you can determine what sounds resonate with what chakra on an individual basis.

PROTECTIVE SHEATH

When the chakras are open, as they are after a balancing, the client is vulnerable to the entry of negative energy. To guard against this eventuality, it is necessary to protect the energy centres by encasing them in some form of protection. "Applying a protective sheath" can best be achieved by using an analogy the client understands, such as slipping into a sleeping bag and doing up the zipper, if the person is the outdoor type; or if making clothes is understood, then have a bolt of material wrap itself around them from top to bottom.

Personally, I use a pure white ribbon, six inches wide, which starts at my feet and wraps me up, feet first, followed by my ankles, legs, thighs, around my body, including my hands and arms, my shoulders, right up to my neck, my head and eventually above my head, and then the same process is repeated going downwards over my body. I consider I am now insulated inside my "mummy" like structure, and no negative energy can get to my open chakras.

YES/NO RESPONSES (DOWSING)

Mention was made earlier about the importance of receiving messages, even if this only comes as a "YES" or "NO" answer, although it is preferable that you develop your inner senses to receive more complete information. The simplest method of receiving Yes/No answers involves the use of a crystal - usually a single terminated quartz, suspended from a chain with some type of catch or hook on the "blunt" end. A chain is passed through the hook and by holding the chain in one hand, the crystal is allowed to swing freely, pointing downwards. By placing the palm of your other hand under the point of the crystal (quite close), the crystal will move, usually backwards and forwards, or sometimes in a circular motion. It may be necessary to adjust the distance from the point of the crystal to the palm of the hand to obtain the full and obvious movement, which is governed by which body is affecting the crystal the most.

You may think the hand holding the chain is causing the movement, but if you steady yourself, you will see that you are not. Bring the movement of the crystal to rest, i.e. a stationary position but still suspended above the palm. To establish what movement signifies a "yes" response and a "no" response, ask a question in your mind to which you know the answer, such as "Do I own a Holden motor car?" (or whatever type of car you have). The crystal will move, given a few seconds to half a minute. Note the direction of the movement. Now ask yourself another question ("Do I own a Rolls Royce?") and it should move in a different way, unless of course you are lucky enough to own both a Rolls Royce and a Holden or whatever car you own. The movement may be a North-South movement followed by an East-West movement, or it may be circular clockwise movement, followed by circular anti-clockwise movement, or any other combination which clearly differentiates the two answers.

Although you know what cars you own without asking the crystal, by asking questions where the answer is known by you, it is more likely you can accept that the crystal can respond to your thought questions. You can therefore have confidence asking other questions to which the answers are not known to you, for example "Am I deficient in Vitamin C?"; or "Is it appropriate that I buy ......?". There is the situation of course where there is no straight-forward "yes" or "no" answer, which means we need to understand how the crystal shows us a "don't know". The simplest way around this is to ask the crystal to show you a "yes', a "no", and a "don't know" each time you start a session. With a little practice, you will find your crystal happily providing information about vitamins, minerals, colors, vibrations and anything else that can be of benefit to you. If you want to read more about it before trying it for yourself, you will find a detailed description covered in many books including, *Discover Crystals* by Ursula Markham. A clean crystal should be used, and details of "cleansing" are included in the section under that name.

COLORS and SOUND

Our physical bodies are made up primarily of liquid, and are affected by both sound and color vibrations. Each of us vibrates at a unique rate, in much the same way as we have a unique set of fingerprints or DNA. The vibration frequency of each of our individual bodies is a "composite" vibratory rate of all the parts of our body. As we are affected by sound and colors, I find no difficulty in accepting that we can be deficient in a specific color or vibration. This deficiency can be ascertained using dowsing described above. From the point of view of being able to detect the deficiency without dowsing, I cannot do it. I also find it difficult to tell if there is any change when I take remedial action. This is not in any way to suggest that there is no difference, only that I cannot tell the difference. Perhaps in time I will become more sensitive, and will be aware of the deficiency position and the balanced position. In the mean time, I am happy to accept that I should have my physical as well as my other bodies in balance, and will continue to take whatever steps are necessary to ensure that situation. There are several very good articles on this subject, but if you are planning to buy Ursula Markham's book, *Discover Crystals*, (details above), you will find a good explanation in it.

INDIVIDUAL'S COLOR

Each of us has a color in our make up with which we are most connected, and for many of us it will be the color associated with our birth-sign. If compatible with our physical body, we should use the gem or crystal that carries "our" ray, which will cause our various bodies to be uplifted and nourished, enhancing our strength, vitality, energy, and being. The color and vibrations will contribute to our strength and balance, which in turn will enhance the function of all of our faculties. Each color ray has an associated sound and vibratory rate which is detailed in chapter 2 "Chakra Points and Balancing".

MEDITATION

Meditation has been practiced in the Eastern countries for thousands of years. It gains and wanes in popularity in our Western civilisation and is currently continuing an upsurge which began thirty years ago. Meditation enables a person to be more in touch with the higher self. Meditation stills the mind, allowing connection with internal sources, and in so doing reduces the pressure of work, alleviates pain, fights illnesses, and assists in assessing your future direction, and so on. Regular meditation calms or stills the mind, opening it to "the other world", which is a necessary element for those seeking to increase their psychic awareness. Whilst it takes time to meditate, the investment of time makes the remainder of the day more productive and capable of being more usefully employed.

I will describe two types of meditation, where the primary difference is the time frame involved and in the depth of meditation achieved. One can be completed quite quickly, in say 10 - 20 minutes, whereas the deeper form takes about an hour. It may be useful to attempt both before deciding which is more appropriate for you. When we meditate, our brain waves slow down. There are four ranges of brain waves, namely Beta waves (approx 12 - 25 cycles per second), Alpha waves (8 - 15), Theta waves (3 - 9) and Delta waves (0.5 - 4). In the alert state, (Beta waves) our brain gives off small amplitude, relatively rapid waves, and as we relax, Alpha waves take over which are larger in amplitude but slower in frequency. In the Theta range, the amplitude increases further, and we are more relaxed again. In the Delta range, our brain is giving off the largest amplitude and slowest frequency waves of all brain activity.

The range of each type of brain waves overlap a little, depending on the individual, so we will all act a little differently, but as a general rule, meditation takes place in the Theta and Delta ranges. It will take longer to reach a Delta condition than a Theta condition for any given individual, as we go through each stage as our brain "slows down". When brain activity slows down, the left and right halves of the brain come into synchronisation, and both are used simultaneously. This does not occur in the Alpha or Beta ranges, where we are most of the time. It is in this "slowed down" state that meditation can take place, although we continue to have Alpha and/or Beta brain wave activity.

Some practitioners recommend daily or more frequent meditation, while others consider that every second or third day is sufficient. The shorter duration variant is more suited to daily use, with the longer one more suited to once or twice weekly, although there is no doubt that the more frequently meditation is practiced the better. Before discussing meditation itself, it is appropriate to make a few suggestions which may help make meditation easier. The "right" surroundings are perhaps the most obvious and include a quiet location where no one will call in on you unannounced, and if you have a phone, let the answering machine answer it for you, or turn it down so you are not aware if it rings. A shawl or a blanket for wearing around your shoulders or to sit on, or have over your lap, is useful, as is a darkened room, although it is not necessary if the light coming in does not change substantially.

Meditative music serves various purposes, including slowing down your brain waves subliminally, and helps eliminate outside noise. Tapes or disks specifically for the purpose of meditation are readily available and one of the leading sources of this material is The Synchronicity Foundation, who have a wide range of meditative music on tape, with graded programs to suit most people. Another excellent range on both tape and CD is provided by Tony O'Connor, a Queensland musician. Details are in the appendix. Crystals also play a valuable part in meditating by increasing the depth and extent of meditation. Typically, quartz crystals are used, although some people prefer to use a gemstone which has an association for them personally; perhaps a gift from a loved one; a birthday stone; or maybe one that was "found" and is there for that purpose. You may wish to refer to the earlier section on getting your own crystal/gemstone in chapter 2. A list of zodiac associated gems is listed in chapter 5, and Gemstones and Associations with Physical Ailments (chapter 6) under meditation, may provide you with some ideas.

With the setting "right", we are now ready to meditate, to be open to contact from sources outside our own "world" from whom we may obtain information. The first step in getting in touch with spirits greater than us is to firstly reach inside ourselves for our deepest, innermost thoughts. We are going to have a period of time, from five minutes to half an hour, when we are calm, relaxed, deep in thought, with appropriate music and perhaps holding our crystal or gemstone, where we literally open our mind up to receive anything that any one wants to send us, including our own spirit guides. Initially, we will be bombarded by our own thoughts and I do not believe we can avoid this, although with perseverance, it can be controlled, allowing more significant information to reach us.

I set the scene by lighting my incense burner and/or candles about ten or fifteen minutes before settling down, ensuring the flames are out of reach in case I knock them over. I find it useful to have a pen and paper close at hand for use at the end of the meditation session. I have a regular place to sit, and because it is easy to fall asleep during meditation, I believe it is better to sit than lie down. I sit up straight, shawl around my shoulders, my feet on the floor, legs and feet straight, not crossed, hands in my lap, facing upwards, my left hand holding my crystal pointing upwards. This groundwork prepares my mind for meditation, and I am half way there as soon as I sit down. A common alternative is to sit on the floor with legs crossed, and you should consider trying both methods to see which suits you best.

I commence by closing my eyes, and start to breathe deeply and regularly, in and out, quite slowly. I count my breaths in as 1, out as 2, in as 3, out as 4, and so on, and by concentrating on the numbers and breathing deeply, I feel a "pressure" or "buzz" at the top of my head within a few minutes. I continue counting and breathing, with the counting preventing me from letting my mind wander.

I will now describe two alternatives you may wish to try. The ending to both types of meditation is the same, and is described after the second method.

The "FIVE MINUTE" meditation.

Although I call it the five minute meditation, you can make it ten, fifteen, or twenty minutes, - whatever suits you. After five minutes or so, of breathing as described, and encouraging my mind to become still, I usually experience little flashes of light darting across my closed eyes. Sometimes they are balls of color, perhaps a purple, which gets larger and larger, and fills my entire view. Within that color, there in normally another ball, perhaps of a different color. If it is the same color, there is a short time separation. Each one continues to move in the same direction and speed as the previous one, and the process continues.

If the image is not balls of color, it may be a building, a gemstone, the shape of an object, perhaps a car, some food, a person, or an event, that hangs there for a moment or two. Occasionally it just fades away, at other times it moves out of my vision to the right or left and it is often replaced by another shape, and these shapes build up a little story. The images, whether they are colors, shapes, events, or anything else, all combine to tell me something from either deep within me or from another source. When I finish the meditation, I spend some time making sense of the sequence of pictures. In the beginning, my stories appeared to be a jumbled and disjointed sequence of events that did not make sense, but with experience I can now make out a meaningful story in most of them. It would be helpful if someone close to you is psychic is some way, for, as with dream interpretation, it takes a little practice to see the meaning, but persevere, as it is worth it. The end result is much like dreaming, but can be recalled and analysed more easily.

The "DEEPER TRANCE" meditation.

In this variation, I spend the first five minutes as before, but continue to concentrate on breathing deeply. I let the air fill my lungs, and rather than consciously exhale, I drift into just letting my lungs empty with no effort from me. I imagine the breath entering through my nostrils, down the back of my throat, into my lungs, and after a minute or so, I imagine the flow of air moving inside me. I focus on this and find my head becoming a little lighter. I imagine my lungs to be a long thin, transparent, bicycle pump, located at my back in the spinal area, and the air fills this chamber, and then empties it. I can visualise the level of air in the chamber as I inhale and exhale.

I continue to breath deeply, and consciously push the air all the way down and out of the bottom of the chamber, right down to my diaphragm, and then I let it come out again. I find it easier to start with the air going into the lungs, but more effective when I shift it lower in the body. I visualise oxygen invigorating my blood, benefiting all parts of my body. After five minutes or so have passed, I have usually forgotten about counting, although I do not consciously stop counting. I just lose track of the conscious effort and then I realise that I am not counting any more. I exhale once or twice more then breath less deeply, letting my breathing become unconscious again.

I point my eyes to the top of my head, imagine both halves of my brain, and visualise the walnut appearance of each part. I make a connection between them, by imagining a road bridge running from one side to the other, allowing the ideas of one to be shared by the other. Across that bridge, I imagine a huge neon arrow, with points in each direction, indicating that traffic can flow in both directions. When I get to this point, I can virtually "feel" the connections being made in my head, between the two halves of my brain. There is a "buzzing" going on, and thoughts pop into my mind. I focus on the arrow and bridge, and see imaginary messages moving across the bridge, going backwards and forwards, and I tell my mind to "be still", pause, "be still", pause, "be still", I find that I do not actually think of anything, other than "being still". I gradually reduce the frequency of telling my mind to be still, and continue with my focus on the flow of information across the bridge.

I would like to say that my mind stays blank, but it does not, and before I know it, I am thinking about something of this world. It is a little while before I realise it, and rather than get frustrated about it, I take a mental note of the subject, and tell my mind, that I will look at this subject after the meditation. That seems to satisfy whatever part of me brought the subject to my notice. I have recognised the subject, agreed to handle it later, and I go back to "being still". Over a period of time, I find that I drag up ten or more such subjects, and by now it is becoming obvious to me what has the higher priority. I then focus with all my faculties on that subject trying to see why it has been raised, what solutions are available, the effects of each, alternative strategies and so on. I explore at length each of the options, try to see the effect on any one involved, whether there is a better alternative, what is morally right, what is more timely, more appropriate, another way of looking at the same element, and investigate each sub-option of each part of each potential solution.

Having fully concentrated on the one subject, the rest of my mind stills itself, and I address the immediate problem. At some point in that cycle, I exhaust all the alternatives and just sit there, not thinking of anything. It does not last for long before something else pops into my head again, but as I practice, the time, a few seconds initially, appears to increase, but I cannot really be sure, as I am not focussed on it. Before I know it, my CD player has stopped, and I realise that I have been in this state for some considerable time, at least 60 minutes. Interestingly enough, my mind must have been switching from "thought" to "blank" quite often, because the hour is reached much more quickly than would seem reasonable. This is normally confirmed by my doing something, or not doing something, which is out of character, but turns out to be right for me. I have obviously been processing something I am not consciously aware of, and assume it happened during my meditation.

ENDING MEDITATION

In an unhurried way, I bring myself back to conscious awareness in the room where I am meditating. I see the room in my mind; the seats, the carpet, the hi-fi, the tables and so on. I stretch my fingers and hands, my neck, and sometimes, my feet and legs. I do this slowly over a period of a minute or two, slowly open my eyes and come back to the physical world. In the case of the five minute meditation, I note down the parts of the story on my pad, and spend a few minutes analysing what the message is about. In the case of the deeper trance meditation, I thank my unconscious mind for helping me explore the many options available to me, and thank myself for having the courage and resourcefulness to be as strong as I need to be, to be true to myself. I always spend a few minutes before rising, thinking about the points that were raised during my meditations this ensures that I have kept my side of the bargain, and looked at the problems raised. I do not worry so much about getting the solution, just to consciously address the problem, realise that some part of me thinks there is a problem, and that I recognise it. That is, after all, what I promised to do, so it is adequate to that, and nothing else.

When I get up, I blow out the candles, remove my shawl and put it away, and always have something to drink. I usually remember to turn on the door buzzer and check the answering machine. I feel relaxed and believe that I have achieved benefit for the time invested. My advice to you when meditating is to try and remember it is not a competition. There are no prizes for being able to go deeper, be there longer, achieve more, or anything of the sort. The level of meditation you achieve is appropriate for you at this stage of your development. If you accept that, you will ENJOY yourself. Try not to make it hard work.

OTHER FORMS OF MEDITATION

Although not necessarily recognised as meditation, being actively absorbed in painting, composing, writing and gardening all qualify as meditation. The act of focus and concentration involved is very similar to the activities described above, and the same feeling of getting in touch can take place. Individuals who are hyperactive may benefit from this process as a stepping stone to the more formal methods outlined.

Realising that the above methods may not suit everybody, you will be able to find lots of books on meditation, with each author having their own favourite technique for meditating. For instance, in the book *Discover Crystals* by Ursula Markham, she outlines about half a dozen alternatives, one of which may suit you if mine does not. Another method is discussed in *The Healing Power Of Crystals* by Magda Palmer. Try the different methods you read or hear about, until you find one that suits you.

DIVINATION

The definition of DIVINATION according to one encyclopedia is the practice of trying to learn about the unknown by magical or supernatural means. Within this general heading is included dowsing, necromancy, astrology, dream interpretation, palmistry, tea leaf readings, crystal ball gazing, tarot cards, and others. The word appears to satisfy nearly anything of a supernatural nature. For the purposes of this book, my more narrow meaning of divination refers to attempting to predict the future based on what gems a person selects from a group, their individual significance and their relationship with each other. The skilled practitioner will interpret the significance of the clients selection, including which gems are not selected, or are handled before rejection.

In many ways there are similarities with Tarot readings, but on this occasion the individual looks at a tray of gems and selects a nominated number, usually 7, 9 or 11. As each gem is selected, it is placed on a cloth, which can contain markings or can be plain. An analysis follows, based on the order of choice, which gems were handled before being rejected, where the selected items are placed on the material, direction if appropriate, proximity to each other, size, side facing up, as well as the choice of the gems themselves. Although I am still learning this technique, it excites me greatly, as I believe the selection displays a degree of unconscious knowledge. I have not yet deduced, nor have I received psychic advice as to interpretation to be used, but I am practising at my own pace and consider it likely that I will develop this form of foretelling the future.

The information that I have suggests that you, as the "reader" or interpreter for your client, should chose each of the gems yourself, or at least the bulk of them, after considering the significance of each. I do not believe there is any value in coming home with a box of fifty or one hundred gems and then trying to determine the properties of each. You should select a range of gems that include your personal interpretation of what each will do. For example, if you chose a rose quartz or two, you may be doing so in the knowledge that whoever selects it is in need of healing from some sort of hurt. Another person choosing rose quartz may believe, and to them it represents a true belief, that it indicates that the client will assist another to get over a traumatic experience. Neither is necessarily right or wrong, but your vibes and belief system will be in your gems, and the client will be affected when he/she makes the selection.

As a starting point in assisting with the properties of each, it is possible to use the benefits and concerns expressed in chapter 3 - "Details on selected Crystals & Gems". These will be valid to some degree, and you can determine exactly which way, as well as the relationship between two or more different gems. Again as an example, as interpreted by you, a green aventurine placed close to rose quartz may indicate that deep healing is taking place already, whereas to someone else, it may indicate that it is now even more necessary and urgent. As you use your gems, you will develop your intuitive process and may modify your understanding of each gem. At the outset, you may find it useful to have a chart handy with key words displayed for each gem, and perhaps relationships of the more important, although you will soon discard this in favour of your intuitive process. As I indicated above, I am relatively new to this form of using gems, but I will be pursuing it and will include additional details in future releases of this book and disk.

MINERAL WATER - (GEM ELIXIR)

Mineral water is obtained by water passing through different minerals as it rises to the surface of the earth, and the result is a bubbly, pleasant drink. It is available in both commercial and "do-it-yourself" springs. Many people claim beneficial effects from drinking mineral water collected direct from springs, ranging from relief from rheumatism to cures for insanity. Crystal mineral water is created by the immersion of crystals and gems into a filled water container to let the healing power of the crystals be absorbed into the water, although the water does not become effervescent. The water can then used for drinking, diluting into medicine, feeding to plants, for use in fish aquariums, or for bathing oneself. Because of its method of production, it is sometimes referred to as "elixir" or "gem elixir".

The process is the same regardless of which gems or crystals are used. The gems or crystal are placed in a container which is filled with filtered water if possible, as tap water is now contaminated with fluoride and chlorine as well as many other minerals and trace elements. The water jar and crystals are left at least overnight, but for a longer period of 2 - 4 days if possible. The water can then be taken directly, or can be diluted, depending on the mineral used, with similar results being achieved. The benefits that are associated with the crystal or gem used, will be in the water and can reinforce the action of handling or wearing the gem. In ancient times, there was a belief that the gems should be ground up and taken as a powder, although there is now more reason to believe that the beneficial effects can be achieved without such a permanent end to the gems concerned.

The water can be flavoured if desired, can be used for tea or coffee making, cooking, used to water plants, fish bowls, for ice cubes, and so on, with the beneficial effects being retained. Care should be taken not to leave crystals and/or gems in the water indefinitely, as their power will be drained. Being sensitive to the gems will ensure they are not over-used, and if appropriate several group of gems can be used providing the opportunity of receiving all of their beneficial qualities. In future releases of this book, I will provide more explicit instructions regarding the use of elixirs, their most appropriate use and strength.

THE AURA.

Everyone has emotions, thoughts, memories, and something I shall call the subconscious. Some people are also aware of intuition. We are all aware of our physical body and I find it easy to accept that a body of similar shape exists an inch or two out from the physical, and another an inch or two out from that, and another, and another. The body closest to the physical is the etheric body, the energy field which surrounds the physical body, followed by the emotional body, which influences our feelings towards others. Further out again is the mental body, which stores memories, where patterns of the past are kept. Further out still is the subconscious body, a relatively thin sheath. Still further out is the soul, not properly a body, but spirit. Outside of that is the worlds of The Source, or God as most people think of it, at least initially. The various bodies that surround the physical form what is known as the "aura". In addition to these bodies surrounding the body, there are others which appear above the crown of the head.

Depending on the health of the various bodies of the individual, the colors of each body blend into the next, just as with a rainbow to form a composite "haze" around the physical body, varying in intensity and clarity, and subject to regular changes. Some people can see auras, others cannot, and most of us have had the ability "turned off" by our Western upbringing. Personally I can not see auras, but I am consciously trying to develop the ability again. On one occasion I did see a "halo" or color "outline" around one person, but as it occurred only once, I have to be content that at this stage of my development, auras are not visible to me as they are with some other people. Individuals who see auras can distinguish the individual bands of color, and can tell where one body starts and another finishes.

Although I find the above description acceptable to me, you may find it conflicts with what you feel, so I suggest you take whatever fits most comfortably with you as an individual and merge it into your belief system. You may care to consider for example, that the unconscious mind is in your head or heart, and that your emotional feelings may originate in your heart, or gut, or anywhere that makes sense to you. The book by Joseph Ostrom entitled *You And Your Aura* covers this aspect in much more detail.

REINCARNATION

Most individuals who get involved in alternative lifestyles, have usually set about looking for something other than the conventional, and the result of their search depends on the expected outcome and their current level of understanding. Most of the people I talk to simply accept that reincarnation is a "fact of life", if you'll pardon the pun. Personally speaking, I believe that I have been here on this earth many times before, and have chosen to re-incarnate this time in order to carry out some specific purpose, the details of which are not fully known to me at present. All of the tools and help needed are provided as I explore to find out my mission, although I am only presented with enough to move one step at a time. I believe I reincarnated this time to work with crystal healing in some way, and although that is where I am at present, I believe I will become interested in other areas in due course.

A very useful, easily-read book that assisted my understanding of reincarnation is *The Force*, by Stuart Wilde. If you want to understand one persons perspective on the subject, you may find it useful.

MEDIUMS

A medium is a person who assists another to contact someone in the spirit world. This typically would be by way of a seance or similar means and can be either private or in a group. Spiritualists believe the medium gives off a mist-like substance called ectoplasm, which can be moulded by spirits to form hands or vocal chords, or other organs, to use in communicating, although this is not proven. Visiting a medium is generally undertaken to contact a specific spirit, although sceptics may visit to see if they consider it is real or an elaborate hoax.

A good medium passes onto the client information from the spirit world received via feelings, auditory or visual reception, spelling, writing or symbolistic. To be of benefit, the client should feel that the meeting of the spirit and physical world actually took place and was beneficial in some way, even if only to put ones mind at rest. I found the book *Reaching For The Other Side* by Dawn Hill very interesting.

CHANNELLING

In a similar manner to the medium, a channeller contacts someone in the spirit world, often their spirit guide. In some instances it is a spirit who has returned to help in a specific way, for example to take on the responsibility for assisting with the development of crystal awareness, or the survival of the dolphin species, or the power of the earth to renew itself. In the case of a single spirit channeller as they are called, there is a air of "mission" or "crusade". They have often returned and will speak to many people, often through one channeller, and endeavour to recruit many appropriate souls to carry out the task. Several spirits have been active for a period of ten or twenty years laying the ground work for the task they accepted and are implementing.

When a visit to a channeller is undertaken, it is often established through the spirit guide of the channeller. Although it is possible to seek contact with someone specific, it is more common to seek the advice of the spirit guide to clarify direction, seek understanding or assistance with an event or series of events here on earth. The spirit guide communicates the answer through the channeller.

As mentioned the book *Reaching For The Other Side* by Dawn Hill is very interesting.

CRYSTAL & GEMSTONE THERAPY

There is a great deal of information available in relation to which crystals and gemstones are good for certain ailments or for the prevention of certain conditions, although much of it appears contradictory. Although I am sure that the information is provided by the various authors in good faith, one book may state that amethyst will assist problems of a broken heart, whereas another suggests that it is beneficial for opening up an other perspective. I have not yet found any information which offers strong advice AGAINST using a particular gemstone, although a cautionary note about the extreme outcomes that may be encountered with some, is occasionally included. These largely warn the uninitiated to be aware of the potential outcome and to be ready to respond accordingly. There is general agreement among authors about the positive results that are achieved by the use of crystals and gemstones.

HEALING.

Crystals can heal! Do not let anyone tell you they cannot. There are as many healing methods as there are healers, with most competent healers having developed their own procedures. It is up to every individual to determine what feels comfortable to them and to develop a healing system that satisfies their own personal values. I have attended many workshops where healers place crystals and/or gems on the client with great success. Others, who appear to be equally successful, do not put any gems on the clients body at all, but rather use their hands, with or without holding a crystal. Still others use a mixture of both, again with apparent success.

If you wish to perform healing for others, you may consider visiting existing healers and/or attending their workshops, until you find an acceptable form of healing. From my own point of view, I like to "have a chat" with my clients before I attempt anything. This may last for only a few minutes or may last for up to an hour. I feel that unless I have some idea of what frame of mind they are in, and what they expect, I am potentially wasting my time. At the end of our "chat", I know to a reasonable degree, what they perceive their problem to be, and how they will be able to tell if an improvement is effected. Armed with this information, I ask them to lie down on a healing table and have them do a short meditation. (Before my clients arrive, I have arranged continual CD music of an appropriate nature, have either candles or the incense burner alight, have sought the assistance of the healing powers of the Crystals, and have charged the room with positive energy. The majority of clients comment that the room has a lovely feeling when they first enter).

I use a crystal suspended on a chain positioned one to six inches out from the clients body and initially move around them quite slowly. I am looking for the crystal to move in some way, either in or out, or from side to side, as I maintain the crystal within their aura. I start at the head, progress down the right side, up the left side, then over the face and torso. Having completed the circuit over their body and noted areas of change, I now concentrate on any areas where abnormal movement occurred. Holding a male crystal in my right hand, point toward the client, I focus on each of the areas indicated, sensing the change within the crystal as I move through each of the various bodies, until I am sure which body is in need of repair. By either circling the spot on the body, or moving in a criss cross fashion, I activate the energy in the immediate vicinity until the feeling abates, usually taking a minute or two, but sometimes longer, continuing until I believe no more action is required. I then move onto the next spot, and continue the process. Sometimes I feel the need to ask the client to roll over and work on their back as well, but only do this if my inner voice tells me to do so. When prompted to, I discuss the potential blockage with the client as I work, otherwise I wait until I am finished, when I have a more complete picture.

In as many as a third of my healings, I feel the need to place a gemstone on a given area of the clients body after working on a particular spot, so that additional healing can continue to take place while I work on other parts of the client. This is the only time I actually touch the client, and I advise them beforehand, asking permission for what I am about to do. I have a reasonably wide range of gemstones, and use them as described in the following chapter, "Details on Selected Gems and Crystals". On occasions, the gemstones placed on the body roll off, and I accept that it has been on for long enough, or maybe should not have been put on in the first place. In either case, I leave it off, telling the client what is going on and continue with the healing. When I have finished the healing, I do a chakra balancing of all the chakras, whether or not any was involved in the above process. I then request the client to remain on the healing table and tell me what they experienced. We discuss this and I might bring into the conversation something like "you seem to be bottling up some emotional matter in your solar plexus area, are you experiencing some sort of emotional upset"? or whatever I have detected. We then expand the discussion to explore that subject. I find it very useful to have the client "open up" at this time, to get the full benefit of the healing. In some cases the client finds this disclosure upsetting, others take it in their stride, and in either case, we continue until there is no more to be gained.

Lastly, but very importantly, before the client sits upright, I have them cover themselves with the "protective sheath" described earlier, as their body would otherwise be liable to be invaded by negative energy when they leave the room. (The world is full of negative energy, looking for somewhere to go). Whatever crystals or gems have been used, I put aside for cleaning, as they may have picked up the clients negativity and I do not want to pass it onto anyone else. Although I have described what I do, it is not so much the process as the intent that is important. Unless you want to assist your client for the best possible reasons, (and that is not financial), it is unlikely you will succeed. Love, peace, and sensitivity to another persons needs should be paramount. By asking the crystals to assist you, and leaving the rest to the universe, the right outcome will probably be achieved, whether you agree with it or not.

USING THE DETAILED LIST OF CRYSTALS AND GEMS

I have endeavoured to produce a list of crystals and gemstones and their properties that makes sense to me, and these are listed in the following chapter. If I differ from others, it is because I believe that this is what I have been told to pass on. I intend to provide updated information that will increase the quantity and quality of information about the gems with which I come into contact. I will provide details of new and different stones, and any time I find that current information is incomplete, I will update it or described it more clearly. It is my intention that you, the reader of this book or disk, have the most up to date and current information available.

I suggest you use the various gems as described, after reading the information provided. If a particular gemstone is not achieving the expected results, change to another. It is as simple as that, CHANGE. Changing can do you no harm if the existing pattern is not doing what you expect. An alternative may work and it is worth a try, as I believe the gems around us are available to help. If you hold a tiger's eye and think it will calm you down, it probably will, even though other people may think rose quartz would do it better. Tiger eye, or any other gemstone, is not going to get you more enraged just because you do not know enough to choose the ideal stone.

Choosing the right stone is a function of your personal level of expertise, and as you gain knowledge through personal experience, you will choose more appropriately for each given situation. If you have a gem you are not familiar with, close your eyes and ask if that stone is appropriate for the job at hand, listen to your inner self, and act on the answer. It is desirable that you develop your inner feelings so that you can detect when you are being "told" something. Even if you only "think" you are being told something, accept it, act on it, and if necessary ask for a clearer message next time, explaining that you are not as good at deciphering your feelings as you would like, but are eager to learn.

If you do not get any answer, one technique that you may consider is color association, which utilises the same color stone as the color of the chakra that you are addressing, and the best possible result in the circumstances will be achieved. (See chapter 2 - "Chakra Points and Balancing" or chapter 6 - Physical Ailments). I do not know of any healer who is not still learning after many years of healing. Most of us are at the high learning end of the curve, others who have been involved for many years are at the more subtle end, where they continue to hone their skills.

Crystals are prepared to work with

us when we are ready

Agate
Color: Various colors with bands and stripes. Associated colors: Blue.

Agate affects both the physical and mental processes. A grounding but energising stone. Assists in developing memory, courage, an acceptance of truth and a realisation of things for what they are. Blue Lace Agate engenders calmness in the mind, Moss Agate acts on the heart, immune system and lungs, Fire Agate brings focus and acceptance of situation.

Caution: Bright blues and greens are probably died and shouldn't be used.

Types: Tumble polished, cabochons.

Wearing: Differing colored gems work on different chakra's.

Chakra points affected: BL and Fire - Base; Moss - Heart.

Cleansing: Rock salt bath.

Naturally Occurring: Eur., India, N. Amer., S. Amer.

Derivation: From the river Achates in Southern Italy.

Frequency: Widespread.

Bodies affected: Physical, Mental.

Birthstone Information;
Zodiac dates: December 23 - January 19.
Zodiac sign: Capricorn, the goat.
Ruler of House: 10th.
Ruled by: Saturn.
Associated Stones: Agate (Fire), Smoky Quartz.
Associated Color: Brown, Black.
Associated Metal: Lead.
Associated Plant: Ivy, Pansies.
Associated Tree: Pine, Elm, Poplar.
Associated Country: India, Mexico.
Associated Cities: Delhi, Oxford.
Element: Earth.
Body Area: Knees.
Characteristics: Ambitious, cautious, patient, persistent.
Wedding anniversary gift for: Fourteenth.

Alexandrite

Color: Emerald green in daylight, red in artificial light. Associated colors: Green.

Assists in rebuilding and aligning the physical, mental and emotional bodies in a sensitive manner. Affects the bodies nervous system, spinal column, and liquid carrying organs. Those spiritually receptive will receive renewed growth and understanding. Balancing stone, providing inner peace.

Types: Facets, cabochons, tumble polished.

Wearing: Crown, neck.

Chakra points affected: Crown.

Duration: Can be worn all the time if comfortable.

Cleansing: Rock salt bath.

Naturally Occurring: Africa, Eur., S. Amer.

Derivation: Czar Alexander II of Russia.

Frequency: Rare.

Bodies affected: Physical, Emotional, Mental.

Amazonite

Color: Green or blue/green. Associated colors: Blue.

Puts mind at rest, soothes nerves. Puts ones own actions into perspective, making release of negative attitudes easier. Provides ability and strength for mind and body to rebuild, bringing acceptance and satisfaction. Assists in alignment of various bodies, especially mental and spiritual. Those who are creative will benefit from additional new ideas that will develop, especially in difficult situations. Beneficial to those who are dying, as transition is eased.

Types: Cabochons.

Wearing: Neck.

Chakra points affected: Throat.

Cleansing: Running water.

Naturally Occurring: Africa, Eur., India, S. Amer., N. Amer.

Derivation: Named after the Amazon river.

Frequency: Rare.

Bodies affected: Physical, Mental, Spiritual.

Amber (Succinite)
Color: Pale yellow to reddish yellow. Associated colors: Orange.

Influences physical body, especially the chest area, asthma type ailments, and liquid carrying organs. Brings to the surface feelings that can benefit from the healing and soothing effect of both the emotional and spiritual bodies. Absorbs negativism, calms nerves, aids the healing process, provides uplift in times of depression. Makes one more aware of deeper meaning for personal activities and objectives. Assists in setting perspective's and balancing positive and negative feelings.

Types: Usually Resin drops, but also as facets and cabochons.

Wearing: Wear close to the heart, or carry in blouse or shirt pocket. Duration: Do not wear continuously. Give both the wearer and Amber a break.

Chakra points affected: Heart, solar plexus, spleen.

Cleansing: Running water.

Naturally Occurring: Eur.

Derivation: Urgofinnish origin.

Frequency: Common.

Bodies affected: Physical, Emotional, Spiritual.
Birthstone Information;
Zodiac dates: June 23 - July 23.
Zodiac sign: Cancer, the crab.
Ruler of House: 4th.
Ruled by: Moon.
Associated Stones: Amber, Moonstone.
Associated Color: Grey, Green, Silver.
Associated Metal: Silver.
Associated Plant: Wild Flowering Plants.
Associated Tree: Those rich in sap.
Associated Country: NZ, Scotland.
Associated Cities: New York, Venice.
Element: Water.
Body Area: Breasts.
Characteristics: Intuitive, artistic, emotional, irrational.

Amethyst

Color: Lavender, Purple. Associated colors: Indigo, blue.

Ray carried: Violet.

Beneficial to the heart, blood, glands and immune systems. Can assist with problems associated with alcoholism. Amethyst opens the path from the neck to the brow charka's, assisting in the ability to see into the inner world, removing illusions, whilst enhancing channelling and psychic abilities. Provides strong balancing effect on and between emotional, memory, spiritual and physical bodies, bringing spiritual unfoldment. Aids in reducing stress, anger and violence, calms, and is beneficial for meditation. Promotes sleep if put under pillow at night.

Associated stone: Purple rainbow fluorite.

Caution: Do not leave in direct sunlight, as this reduces color.

Types: Crystals, spheres, cabochons, facets, tumble polished.

Wearing: Over heart for connection with emotional body, balancing the inner bodies.

Chakra points affected: Crown, brow, heart.

Duration: Limited use for healing, say 15 - 20 minutes to start with. If sick, use for only 5 minutes at a time.

Cleansing: Rock salt bath.

Naturally occurring: Eur., India, N. Amer., S. Amer.

Derivation: From the Greek "amethystos" - unintoxicating.

Frequency: Rare.

Amethyst - Con't

Bodies affected: Physical, Emotional, Mental, Spiritual.
Birthstone Information;
Birthstone: Pisces.
Zodiac dates: February 20 - March 21.
Zodiac sign: Pisces, the fishes.
Ruler of House: 12th.
Ruled by: Jupiter & Neptune.
Associated Stones: Amethyst, Pearl.
Associated Color: Blue Green.
Associated Metal: Tin.
Associated Plant: Water Lily.
Associated Tree: Willow, Fig, Trees near water.
Associated Country: Portugal.
Associated Cities: Seville.
Element: Water.
Body Area: Feet.
Characteristics: Emotional, intelligent, sensitive, imaginative.

Aquamarine

Color: Light blue and blue/green. Associated colors: Blue.

Aquamarine positively affects the glands, eyes, kidneys and liver, inner aspects, and calms nerves. It balances, removes negativism, brings upliftment by awareness of truth and reality in all aspects of life, providing clear thinking and expression, and realisation of ones potential and self worth. Creative individuals will benefit from wearing Aquamarine during problem solving sessions. Aquamarine given to a dying person will ease the transition to death.

As a result of wearing Aquamarine, rejection of the truth may occur. If it does, it will be necessary to remove the Aquamarine and let realisation of what has been disclosed be accepted. Only then can it be worn again. Eventually, increased inner awareness, greater balance, clear thinking, control and self understanding will be apparent. This in turn will bring harmony and stronger relationships, as well as a clearer spiritual understanding. Physical pain, including grief, can be reduced by wearing blue/green Aquamarine.

Caution: Do not use irradiated crystals, which will cause disharmony, affecting mental and emotional points of view.

Types: Crystals, facets, and rounded.

Wearing: Vary the amount depending on how much inner awareness can be accepted. Most effective worn around the neck or placed on solar plexus.

Chakra points affected: Brow, neck.

Healing: Blue/green Aquamarine affects the physical. Organs which have substances flowing through them can be assisted. (These include heart, liver, spleen, bladder, etc). Reduces fluid retention. Assists eye disorders.

Aquamarine - con't

Duration: As long as can be comfortably tolerated. May be necessary to gradually increase time.

Cleansing: Rock salt bath.

Naturally occurring: Africa, Aust., Eur., India, N. Amer., S. Amer.

Derivation: From the Latin - "aqua" - water, "marina" - marine.

Frequency: Common.

Bodies affected: Physical, Mental.

Birthstone Information;
Zodiac dates: May 22 - June 22.
Zodiac sign: Gemini, the twins.
Ruler of House: 3rd.
Ruled by: Mercury.
Associated Stones: Aquamarine, Tourmaline.
Associated Color: Yellow.
Associated Metal: Mercury.
Associated Plant: Lily of the Valley, Lavender.
Associated Tree: Nut Trees.
Associated Country: USA, Wales.
Associated Cities: London, Melbourne.
Element: Air.
Body Area: Chest, arms and hands.
Characteristics: Clever, curious, expressive, indecisive.

Aventurine

Color: Usually dark or light green, but pink and blue colors also available. Associated colors: Green, pink.

Affects the vital organs within the torso including blood and muscle tissue. Effect is to improve physical health and provide additional resistance against illness. Relieves mental and emotional distortions, provides calming effect, enhances independence, creativity, solves and dissolves problems. Green Aventurine is recognised as one of the great all round "healing stones" bringing balance to troubled or depressed souls, providing encouragement and hope on all levels.

Types: Spheres, cabochons, tumble polished.

Wearing: Dark green around the neck, and light green over the specific area of the body. Dark green color is more powerful.

Healing: Aventurine on its own can repair physical organs. (Light green Aventurine and Emerald to-gether is a more powerful healing force).

Chakra points affected: Heart (green), solar plexus &/or heart (pink), brow (blue).

Duration: Can be worn for as long as it feels comfortable. May take months (or even years for very sick organs) for the effect to become apparent.

Cleansing: Cold water method.

Naturally Occurring: Eur., India, S. Amer.

Derivation: From the Italian "ventura" - accidentally.

Frequency: Rare.

Bodies affected: Physical, Emotional, Mental.

Aventurine - con't

Birthstone Information;
Zodiac dates: October 24 - November 22.
Zodiac sign: Scorpio, the scorpion.
Ruler of House: 8th.
Ruled by: Mars & Pluto.
Associated Stones: Aventurine, Turquoise.
Associated Color: Green.
Associated Metal: Iron.
Associated Plant: Those with dark red flowers, eg Rhododendron.
Associated Tree: Bushy trees, blackthorn.
Associated Country: Norway, Syria.
Associated Cities: Liverpool, Washington, DC.
Element: Water.
Body Area: Sexual Organs.
Characteristics: Aggressive, moody, secretive, leadership.

Azurite

Color: Azure-Blue. Associated colors: Indigo, blue.

Azurite affects the higher energy centres, especially that of opening up the third eye to spiritual awareness. This can lead to a clearer mental perspective and greater self confidence, as well as spiritual unfoldment. It is acknowledged as aid to meditation and psychic awareness, disclosing the individuals higher purpose. Causes fundamental changes to occur, so user should be aware of this fact. Reduces anxiety associated with this world.

Types: Tumble polished, facets, cabochons.

Wearing: Brow and neck.

Chakra points affected: Brow, neck, solar plexus.

Duration: Care should be taken not to flood inner feelings unduly. If uncomfortable, remove and come to acceptance of what has already been revealed, before wearing again.

Cleansing: Rock salt bath.

Naturally Occurring: Africa, Aust, Eur., N. Amer., S. Amer.

Derivation: From the Persian "lazhward" - blue.

Frequency: Common.

Bodies affected: Physical, Mental.
Birthstone Information;
Zodiac dates: November 23 - December 22.
Zodiac sign: Sagittarius, the archer.
Ruler of House: 9th.
Ruled by: Jupiter.
Associated Stones: Azurite, Lapis Lazuli.
Associated Color: Purple.
Associated Metal: Tin.
Associated Plant: Asparagus, Dandelion.
Associated Tree: Lime Oak, Birch.
Associated Country: Australia, Spain.
Associated Cities: Budapest, Cologne.
Element: Fire.
Body Area: Hips and Thighs.
Characteristics: Friendly, relaxed, outgoing, enthusiastic.

Bloodstone (Heliotrope)

Color: Dark Green or Grey/Green with spots of red throughout. Associated colors: Red.

Bloodstone focuses energy to correct out of balance problems in the body. Affects blood circulation, heart, bleeding disorders, the blood, including anaemia, and most organs having liquid passing through them. It elevates physical strength and courage, reduces stress, moderates bad tempers and aggressive behaviour. Increases creativity, self worth and positive outlook. Increases concern for others.

Caution: Can cause physical change by bringing body into balance. If discomfort arises, may be caused by rejection of changes taking place. In this case, remove bloodstone and resolve priorities. Can be used in conjunction with Quartz (Rose or Clear) to diminish effects if too strong.

Types: Cabochons, tumble polished, spheres.

Wearing: Neck and heart.

Healing: Wearer must consciously want healing. Placed over the heart, aids in getting thoughts into perspective, including feelings towards others.

Chakra points affected: Heart, spleen, base.

Duration: Around the neck or heart, as long as comfortable. Over specific area for 1-2 hours per day until change occurs.

Cleansing: Running water method.

Naturally occurring: Aust., China, Eur., India, N. Amer., S. Amer.

Derivation: From the Greek "helios" - sun and "tropos" - turn.

Frequency: Rare.

Bodies affected: Physical, Emotional.

Calcite

Color: Available in green, blue, white/grey, brown, reddish, and many others. Associated colors: Yellow, Orange.

Green Calcite nourishes central body organs, (especially the heart), and bones. Nerves are calmed and more self control provided. The blue variety affects the emotions, and aids in accepting change. White'ish increases self confidence and outlook. In general, calcite brings upliftment and joy on both the mental and emotional levels. Balances emotions, male/female sides, and assists in accommodating change in mental attitudes unconsciously held.

Caution: Affected by water, so don't leave in rain or place in water.

Types: Crystal, facets.

Wearing: Around neck or over spleen.

Chakra points affected: Neck, heart, solar plexus, depending on color used. See general notes on gemstones and colors.

Cleansing: Incense method.

Naturally Occurring: Africa, Aust, Eur, India, N. Amer., S. Amer.

Derivation: From the Latin "calx" - lime.

Frequency: Widespread.

Bodies affected: Physical, Emotional.

Carnelian

Color: Orange or reddish. Associated colors: Orange.

Ray carried: Orange.

Carnelian releases disharmony and disease including toxicity. Aids the blood system, lungs and central body organs, the digestive system, although primary focus is on higher energy centres. Discourages jealous and envious thoughts, replacing them with joyous and contented ones, reduces anger. Stimulates enterprise, concentration, motivation and increases self-sufficiency.

Types: Cabochons, tumble polished.

Wearing: Best worn as a necklace, or over specific organs.

Healing: Carnelian causes the emotions to relax, producing calmer, more balanced outlook. Negative emotions are dulled, dissipated or cancelled out all together. Positive emotions are more easily expressed. Carnelian sharpens, enhances and stimulates mental functions, and in longer term, clarity of thought and accuracy of memory. The improved clarity can cause fundamental change in life. To use, place over the affected area, and let direct sunlight shine on it for 30 minutes. For deeper penetration, use more Carnelian. Carnelian can be used in persistent illnesses, and can also be used in conjunction with Amethyst. Its effects are emphasised if placed over disharmonious area under direct sunlight.

Chakra points affected: Brow, solar plexus, spleen.

Duration: Can be worn once each few weeks. If a sick person, wear each day. If being worn for mental clarity, wear constantly.

Cleansing: Cold water method.

Naturally occurring: Eur., India.

Derivation: From the Latin "corneus" - horny.

Frequency: Common.

Continued overleaf

Carnelian - con't

Bodies affected: Physical, Emotional, Mental.
Birthstone Information;
Zodiac dates: April 21 - March 21.
Zodiac sign: Taurus, the bull.
Ruler of House: 2nd.
Ruled by: Venus.
Associated Stones: Carnelian, Topaz.
Associated Color: Pink, Pale Blue.
Associated Metal: Copper.
Associated Plant: Rose, Poppy - Violet.
Associated Tree: Ash/Cypress, Apple.
Associated Country: Ireland, Switzerland.
Associated Cities: Dublin, Lucerne.
Element: Earth.
Body Area: Throat.
Characteristics: Loving, loyal, possessive, stubborn.

Cassiterite (Tinstone)

Color: Brown, also available in yellow, grey, and black. Associated Color: Yellow.

An all round healer. Works on most chakras, depending on its color. Assists with recovery from physical injury, including blood and bones. It is a grounding stone, balances the emotions, and assisting the wearer to face reality. Engenders a sense of acceptance, a sense of well being. This mineral will become more influential in the future - it has only just started to be understood despite having been mined for hundreds of years.

Types: Faceted, cabochons.

Wearing: Neck.

Chakra Points affected: Uncertain at this stage.

Cleansing: Salt bath method.

Naturally Occurring: Asia, Aust, Europe, N. Amer., S. Amer.

Derivation: From the Greek "Kassiteros" - Tin.

Frequency: Widespread.

Bodies affected: Emotional, Physical.

Celestite

Color: Clear, white, blue. Associated colors: Blue.

Assists the pineal and pituitary glands. Celestite aids mental processes, allowing the more creative aspects to develop. Spiritual growth is encouraged, and astral awareness is heightened. It reduces mental stress, providing a more balanced and defined outlook. In so doing, it may cause change by altering priorities and confidence levels.

Types: Natural, facets, cabochons.

Wearing: Neck.

Chakra points affected: Brow, neck.

Cleansing: Salt bath method.

Naturally Occurring: Africa, Eur., S. Amer.

Derivation: From the Latin "coelestis" - celestial.

Frequency: Common.

Bodies affected: Mental.

Chalcedony

The name given to a variety of crystalline minerals. The group never exhibit any Crystal form however, only occurring as kidney shaped stones. Referred to as the "Mother" stone, generally being associated with love, goodwill, charity. Named after the town of Chalcedon or Kalchidon, in Turkey. Common chalcedony is also know as white Agate. Other varieties include moss Agate, Bloodstone, Carnelian, Chrysoprase, Enhydros, Heliotrope, Jasper, Onyx, Plasma, and Sardonyx. See individual entries for more detail.

Chrysoberyl (see also Alexandrite)

Color: Yellow, green. Associated colors: Yellow.

Chrysoberyl affects the adrenal gland. On the emotional level it increases hospitality towards others, providing a more forgiving attitude. Increases understanding of reasons behind actions, bringing peace of mind. Reduces aggressive behaviour.

Types: Facets, cabochons.

Chakra points affected: Spleen.

Duration: Can be worn for as long as it feels comfortable.

Cleansing: Soak in salt bath for 24 hours and then leave in direct sun for several hours.

Naturally Occurring: Africa, Aust., Eur., India, N. Amer., S. Amer.

Derivation: From the Greek "chrysos" - golden, and the mineral beryl.

Frequency: Rare.

Bodies affected: Emotional, Mental.

Chrysocolla

Color: Blue, green. Associated colors: Blue.

On the physical plane, Chrysocolla aids bone development, keeps physical disorders at bay, particularly female disorders. In an associated sense, it assists men to develop their feminine side. On the emotional and mental levels, helps establish balance, allowing the individual to set and maintain appropriate priorities. Eases pain associated with death and grief. Priorities and understanding become clearer.

Types: Cabochons.

Healing: When worn as a preventative, body will be stronger, resisting physical ailments usually brought about by emotional hang-ups. When worn over heart, will bring joy, upliftment, self confidence.

Chakra points affected: Neck, heart, Solar Plexus.

Cleansing: Running water method.

Naturally Occurring: Africa, Eur., N. Amer., S. Amer.

Derivation: From the Greek "chrysos" - golden, and "kolla" - glue.

Frequency: Common.

Bodies affected: Physical, Emotional, Mental

Chrysoprase

Color: Grey, or greeny/blue. Associated colors: Green, pink, orange.

Balancing stone. Aids in bringing a sense of balance and perspective to the emotional, physical, and mental bodies. Brings into balance both the sexual and the ambition drives at work within us. Enables ones own imperfections and strengths to be realised and reconciled, providing a calmer, less impatient, more rational attitude to everyday life.

Caution: Is considered as a "one person" stone, showing reduced effects for others when previously used by someone else.

Types: Cabochons, tumble polished.

Wearing: As jewellery or carried.

Healing: Works gently to bring awareness of imbalances present in existing patterns. Encourages wearer to undertake change at rate appropriate to their expertise.

Chakra points affected: Brow, heart, base.

Duration: Can be worn as long as it feels comfortable. May be removed to allow changes to consolidate before going on to next priority.

Cleansing: Running water method.

Naturally Occurring: Africa, Aust., Eur., N. Amer., S. Amer.

Derivation: From the Greek "chrysos" - golden and "prason" - to estimate.

Frequency: Rare.

Bodies affected: Physical, Emotional, Mental.

Citrine

Color: Yellow, Orange'ish. Associated colors: Yellow, orange.

Ray carried: Yellow.

Citrine highlights disharmonies in the body, assisting the repair of damaged or unbalanced organs, including kidney, liver, colon, and the blood system including anaemia. Citrine encourages the physical body to relax, and to move into alignment. It benefits any chakra that is partially or fully closed. Inter personal relationships will improve, and responses will become more controllable and rational analysis and conclusions will be more reasoned. Individuals will display a more buoyant attitude to life. Citrine helps individuals become comfortable with the prospect and ramifications of death.

Caution: Much "citrine" is really other members of the quartz family treated in some way, so be careful when selecting.

Types: Crystal, facets, cabochons, tumble polished.

Wearing: Neck, crown, spleen.

Healing: Place citrine over any closed energy centre and it will gradually be opened.

Chakra points affected: Brow, heart, and solar plexus, and others to a lesser degree.

Duration: Citrine can be worn until its effect is evident, then it is only required once each week. It can be worn over any chakra, but for general use should be worn around the neck.

Cleansing: Salt bath or running water methods.

Naturally occurring: Africa, Eur., N. Amer., S. Amer.

Derivation: Named because of its color.

Frequency: Rare.

Bodies affected: Physical, Emotional.

Copper

Color: Brown. Associated colors: Red.

Copper aids the flow of blood, enhancing mind/body connection. Assists in detoxifying body, resists infection, aids in the repair of cuts and abrasions and in arthritic conditions. Provides assistance for physical tiredness, and sexual imbalance.

Types: Crystals made into bracelets etc.

Wearing: Normally worn on wrist or neck.

Healing: Depending on level of disharmony, effect will be felt gradually or almost at once.

Chakra points affected: Heart.

Caution: Copper can cause discoloration of skin and clothing.

Duration: Permanently if required.

Cleansing: Incense method then a commercial cleaner, then leave in sun for one or two hours.

Naturally Occurring: Africa, Aust., Eur., India, N. Amer., S. Amer.

Derivation: From the Latin "cuprum", Cyprus.

Frequency: Widespread.

Bodies affected: Physical

Coral

Color: Black, Pink, Red, White. Associated colors: White, pink, red, fawn.

Differing colors have different strengths. Aids skin, bone and digestive systems, removes negativity and provides access to wisdom and creative forces. Coral works on existing patterns to build a solid base, consolidating this by improving the energy available for life, and maintaining correct balance and outlook.

Caution: Coral is not suitable for everyone, and if you find negativity or restlessness becoming obvious, it should be removed.

Types: Twigs, stems, calcified.

Wearing: As jewellery, carried, or placed around the house or office.

Healing: Differing colors have varying strengths. Red is most powerful, white least so.

Chakra points affected: Neck, heart.

Duration: Initially from 1 - 2 weeks, then for a few hours per day. Can be in aura overnight if comfortable. In children, the elderly and the sick, effect will be noticeable quite soon (2 - 3 weeks), in healthy adults more like 2 - 3 months.

Cleansing: Running water method.

Naturally Occurring: Africa, Aust., Eur., India, N. Amer., S. Amer.

Derivation: From the Greek "korallion" - coral.

Frequency: Widespread.

Bodies affected: Physical.

Wedding anniversary gift for: Thirty-fifth.

Corundum

Corundum is the name given to a group of minerals which include Ruby and Sapphire. See individual gems for details.

Diamond

Color: Clear, through most colors. Associated colors: White, violet.

Diamonds have the ability to assist many ailments, including brain disorders, provide spiritual strength, and create positive feelings in the physical, emotional and mental bodies. It works well with other gemstones, enhancing their power. However, the size of stone needed (2-3 carats minimum) is so expensive to make it virtually unavailable. Aligns oneself with God.

Types: Natural, facets.

Wearing: Anywhere, but fingers & neck most common.

Healing: Diamond is considered as a master healing stone, affecting all charka's. See comment above regarding size. By concentrating on the crown, the brain will focus its effects to the most needy part of the body requiring nourishment and repair.

Chakra points affected: Crown, brow, neck, heart, solar plexus, spleen, base.

Duration: Permanently.

Cleansing: Running water method.

Naturally Occurring: Africa, Aust., Eur., India, N. Amer.

Derivation: From the Greek "adamas" - invincible.

Frequency: Rare.

Bodies affected: Physical, Emotional, Mental, Spiritual.

Continued overleaf

Diamond - con't

Birthstone Information;
Zodiac dates: March 22 - April 20.
Zodiac sign: Aries, the ram
Ruler of House: 1st.
Ruled by: Mars.
Associated Stones: Diamond, Ruby.
Associated Color: Red.
Associated Color: Red.
Associated Metal: Copper.
Associated Plant: Geranium, Honeysuckle, Thistle.
Associated Tree: All thorn bearing trees.
Associated Country: England, France.
Associated Cities: Florence, Naples.
Element: Fire.
Body Area: Head.
Characteristics: Bold, determined, impatient, energetic.

Wedding anniversary gift for: Sixtieth, and seventy-fifth.

Dioptase

Color: Green. Associated colors: Green, red.

Dioptase affects the heart, the nervous system, pineal and pituitary glands. It reduces tension associated with blood pressure, angina and ulcers, providing the individual with a feeling of well being and greater balance. Connects with the spiritual consciousness for development of psychic abilities. Brings good luck and prosperity to the wearer.

Caution: Affected by water, so don't leave in rain or place in water.

Types: Facets, cabochons.

Wearing: Neck, heart.

Chakra points affected: Throat and heart.

Cleansing: Incense method.

Naturally Occurring: Africa, Eur., N. Amer., S. Amer.

Derivation: From the Greek "dia" - through, and "optomai" - vision.

Frequency: Rare.

Bodies affected: Physical.

Emerald

Color: Green. Associated colors: Green.

Ray carried: Green.

Strengthens bones and major body organs, including those carrying blood, the eyes, both physically and psychically. Lifts the state of consciousness of the physical body, stimulates brain activity, resulting in improved memory and emotional outlook, understanding of others and their priorities, and reduces a bad temper. Promotes true, unquestioning love, patience, generosity, compassion.

Types: Facets, cabochons, natural stone, spheres, rondelle.

Wearing: Neck, heart, spleen. The larger the size, or the clearer the stone, the more powerful the gemstone.

Healing: Emerald is known for healing many ailments, but because of its rareness and cost, is not always available to the average person. Dark green Aventurine and Emerald are a powerful healing force for the physical body. They assist in removing pain, both in the head and in specific organs. After the physical body is made whole, Emerald and Quartz over a specific organ will cause resolution of inner body (emotional, mental) problems.

Chakra points affected: Brow, throat, heart.

Duration: Emerald on its own can be worn all the time (24 hours per day).

Cleansing: Running water method.

Naturally Occurring: Africa, Aust., Eur., India, N. Amer., S. Amer.

Derivation: Historical.

Frequency: Rare.

Bodies affected: Physical, Spiritual.

Emerald - con't

Birthstone Information;
Zodiac dates: September 24 - October 23.
Zodiac sign: Libra, the scales.
Ruler of House: 7th.
Ruled by: Venus.
Associated Stones: Emerald, Padparadjah.
Associated Color: Pink, Blue.
Associated Metal: Copper.
Associated Plant: All with Blue flowers, Large roses.
Associated Tree: Ash.
Associated Country: Austria, Japan.
Associated Cities: Lisbon, Vienna.
Element: Air.
Body Area: Kidneys.
Characteristics: Loving, intelligent, pleasant, thoughtful.

Wedding anniversary gift for: Fifty-fifth.

Feldspar

Name given to the group of gems including Amazonite, Labradorite, Moonstone, Sunstone. See individual entries for more detail.

Fluorite

Color: Violet, but also found in green, blue, yellow, brown, red, clear. Associated colors: Indigo, blue.

On the physical body, affects bones, teeth, blood and spleen. On the mental level, develops spiritual awareness. Enhances increased concentration and meditation. Balances Positivity/Negativity. Develops creative and abstract understandings. As with most purple/violet stones, protects the wearer against psychic attack.

Caution: Do not leave in direct sunlight as this reduces color.

Types: Facets, Cabochons.

Chakra points affected: Neck, solar plexus.

Cleansing: Rock salt bath method.

Naturally Occurring: Africa, Aust., Eur., India, N. Amer., S. Amer.

Derivation: From the Latin "fluor" - to flow.

Frequency: Common.

Bodies affected: Physical, Mental.

Garnet

Color: Red. (Green through Orange are available, although not as common). Associated colors: Red.

Garnet strengthens the heart, blood and bone systems, and toxicity. Provides gentle but stimulating action on organs that blood flows through. Aligns mental and emotional bodies with the physical. Balances sexual drive, and encourages self development. On the mental level, provides upliftment and eases depression. Assists in development of creative concepts and ideas.

Types: Facets, cabochons, tumble polished, natural.

Wearing: Heart and neck.

Healing: Can be placed over the affected area or carried on the person.

Chakra points affected: Heart, solar plexus, spleen, base.

Duration: Can be worn continuously if comfortable.

Cleansing: Rock salt bath method.

Naturally Occurring: Africa, Aust., Eur., India, N. Amer., S. Amer.

Derivation: From the Latin "granatum malum" - garnet apple.

Frequency: Common.

Bodies affected: Physical.
Birthstone Information;
Zodiac dates: January 20 - February 19.
Zodiac sign: Aquarius, the water bearer.
Ruler of House: 11th.
Ruled by: Saturn & Uranus.
Associated Stones: Clear Quartz, Garnet.
Associated Color: Blue.
Associated Metal: Uranium.
Associated Plant: Orchids.
Associated Tree: Most fruit trees.
Associated Country: Sweden, Russia.
Associated Cities: Hamburg, Moscow.
Element: Air.
Body Area: Ankles.
Characteristics: Independent, open minded, serious, curious.
Wedding anniversary gift for: Fortieth

Gold

Color: Yellow. Associated colors: Yellow.

Strengthens the physical body, especially the heart and nervous systems. Assists in developing awareness of ones own goals and thought patterns. Wearers are warned that Gold can close the heart to other individuals needs, and to lock themselves into their current state of consciousness.

Types: Natural, and manufactured. The higher the Gold content, the more powerful.

Wearing: Anywhere, but around the heart for maximum benefit.

Chakra points affected: Throat, heart.

Naturally Occurring: Africa, Aust., Eur., India, N. Amer., S. Amer.

Derivation: Historical.

Frequency: Common.

Bodies affected: Physical.

Wedding anniversary gift for: Fiftieth, sixtieth and seventy-fifth.

Haematite

Color: Red, reddish brown, grey. Associated colors: Red.

Affects the blood system and blood disorders, open wounds, the heart, and develops the spleen. Increases energy level and balances physical, mental and emotional bodies. Develops feeling of security, courage and well being. Useful in meditating, as emotional stability is improved.

Types: Facets, cabochons, tumble polished.

Wearing: Neck and heart.

Chakra points affected: Heart, base.

Cleansing: Rock salt bath method.

Naturally Occurring: Africa, Aust., Eur., India, N. Amer., S. Amer.

Derivation: Word means bloodlike.

Frequency: Common.

Bodies affected: Physical.

Heliodore

Color: Yellow.

Affects the blood system and heart. Provides inner calmness in the face of day to day pressures, removing despair associated with the physical world. Aids in aligning the physical and mental bodies.

Types: Facets, cabochons.

Wearing: Neck and heart.

Healing: Wear over the heart for inner strength to cope with pressure; around the neck will saturate aura and benefit the mental outlook.

Chakra points affected: Solar plexus, heart, base.

Cleansing: Rock salt bath method.

Naturally Occurring: Africa, Aust., Eur., India, N. Amer., S. Amer.

Derivation: Word means bloodlike.

Frequency: Common.

Bodies affected: Physical, Emotional.

Indicolite (Indigo or Blue Tourmaline)
Color: Dark blue and blue/green. Associated colors: Indigo.

Indicolite renews life, having a rejuvenating effect. It clarifies aims and dreams, assists in decision making. Indigo absorbs negativity holding individuals back from reaching their full potential. Intuition and psychic awareness are heightened. Promotes an amicable outlook, eases worries and dispels anger.

Types: Facets, cabochons, spheres.

Wearing: Keep in the aura, either by wearing or as a touchstone.

Healing: It will bring to the conscious any disharmony in the physical, emotional, and mental bodies, so they can be removed.

Chakra points affected: Brow, neck.

Cleansing: Rock salt bath method.

Naturally occurring: Africa, Eur., N. Amer., S. Amer.

Derivation: Named after its color.

Frequency: Common.

Bodies affected: Mental.

Ivorite

Color: Light Grey. Associated colors: White.

Brings balance to individuals undergoing change, by slowing down rate of change. Helps to put things into perspective, and provides opportunity to readjust lives. As such, affects mental, emotional, and spiritual as well as physical.

Caution: Do not use with other gems at same time.

Types: Natural, spheres.

Wearing: Around the neck.

Healing: If placed over injury, assists remainder of body to adjust to new situation.

Chakra points affected: Neck.

Duration: Typically 15 minutes over infected area. Can be worn around neck for a week at a time, by which time changes should be evident. Stop wearing for 4 weeks before wearing again.

Cleansing: Running water method.

Naturally occurring: Africa, Aust., Eur., India, N. Amer., S. Amer.

Derivation: Unknown.

Frequency: Rare.

Bodies affected: Physical, Emotional, Mental.

Jade (Jadeite)

Color: Green. Associated colors: Green.

Jade assists those suffering diabetes, whilst Jadeite is more commonly used for muscle strengthening. Both are beneficial for the heart, blood, asthma, the immune system, eye and menstrual disorders. They balance emotions, providing calmness, tranquillity and reduce negativity and clarify decision making. Aids in clear thinking, providing sense of direction and perspective. Jade fosters dreams.

Types: Cabochons, tumble polished.

Wearing: As jewellery, or carried.

Chakra points affected: Brow, neck, heart.

Duration: As long as comfortable.

Cleansing: Salt bath method.

Naturally Occurring: Africa, Aust., Eur., India, N. Amer., S. Amer.

Derivation: From the Spanish "piedra de ijada" - relieving pain in the loins.

Frequency: Rare.

Bodies affected: Physical, Emotional.

Wedding anniversary gift for: Thirty-fifth.

Jasper

Color: Yellow to brown, red to green, depending on inclusions. Associated colors: Yellow, black.

Jasper assists physical healing and eases the pain associated with emotional problems. Whatever variety is chosen, all share those common properties. The Leopard skin variety determines what changes are required in an individual and draws toward them whatever is needed to bring that body into balance. In like manner to attracting what is good for the individual, it rejects what is bad, including other people who would be harmful or have bad intentions. It is therefore potentially beneficial for children. The Poppy variety provides upliftment, inspiration, breaks patterns and blockages. It also assists the blood system. The green variety (as with virtually all green gemstones) heals, and is particularly useful for the heart.

Types: Cabochons, tumble polished, spheres.

Wearing: Generally, around the neck.

Healing: Placed over an area out of balance, it will assist in restoring balance. Particularly useful for the brain, heart and glands (the control centres).

Chakra points affected: Neck - Leopard skin, heart - poppy, green, .

Duration: For attracting balancing needs, wear it continuously. As a healing stone, wear it continuously, or at least for one or two hours each day, until change occurs.

Cleansing: Running water method.

Naturally occurring: Africa, Aust., Eur., N. Amer., S. Amer.

Derivation: Historical.

Frequency: Widespread.

Bodies affected: Physical.

Continued overleaf

Jasper - con't

Birthstone Information;
Zodiac dates: July 24 - August 23.
Zodiac sign: Leo, the lion.
Ruler of House: 5th.
Ruled by: Sun.
Associated Color: Orange, Gold.
Associated Stones: Jasper, Ruby.
Associated Metal: Gold.
Associated Plant: Sunflower, Marigold, Rosemary.
Associated Tree: Orange & all citrus trees, Bay and Palm.
Associated Country: Italy, Rumania.
Associated Cities: Los Angeles, Rome.
Element: Fire.
Body Area: Heart and Spine.
Characteristics: Powerful, proud, energetic, strong-willed.

Kunzite (Pink Spodumene)

Color: Light pink through lavender to yellow. Associated colors: Indigo.

Aids blood, heart, eye and kidneys. Assists with eating disorders and headaches. Will open closed heart chakra. Balances emotional, mental, physical and spiritual bodies. Enhances ability to accept reality, enhances self esteem, provides calming and tolerant attitude toward others. Encourages feelings of security and love. Develops spiritual awareness and growth. A protective gem, keeping at bay negative vibes of others.

Types: Facets, cabochons.

Wearing: Brow, heart.

Chakra points affected: Heart.

Cleansing: Salt bath method.

Naturally Occurring: Africa, N. Amer., S. Amer.

Derivation: George F. Kunz, mineralogist, 1856 - 1932.

Frequency: Rare.

Bodies affected: Physical, Emotional, Mental.

Kyanite

Color: Pale blue. Associated colors: Blue.

Develops creative ability, communication on both the physical and psychical levels. Assists in development of understanding, language, presentation, and ability to express point of view. Spiritual understanding and expression enhanced.

Types: Facets, cabochons, natural.

Wearing: Neck and brow.

Chakra points affected: Brow, neck.

Cleansing: Salt bath method.

Naturally Occurring: Africa, Aust., Eur., India, N. Amer., S. Amer.

Derivation: From the Greek "kyanos" - blue.

Frequency: Common.

Bodies affected: Mental.

Lapis Lazuli (Lazurite)

Color: Royal blue with gold flecks. Associated colors: Indigo, blue.

On the physical level, aids ailments associated with the brain, including depression, although it is genuinely a worker for the higher orders. Assists in revealing inner truths and clarity, and wards off psychic invasion. As a result, a greater sense of confidence and adventure is achieved, tension and anxiety are diminished. Assists in breaking free of past situations, and of attaining mastery over a given situation, of either the mind or body. Opens blocked or closed charkas. Works to bring emotional, mental and spiritual bodies together.

Caution: Do not use dyed stone.

Types: Cabochons, spheres, tumble polished.

Wearing: Wear on brow or around the neck close to the heart. The deeper the color and/or the more gold flecks, the stronger the stone.

Healing: Place over the brow (in headband or scarf), or as earings or short drop pendant.

Chakra points affected: Crown, brow.

Duration: Wear should be restricted to short bursts at beginning, and extended progressively. The longer it is worn, the stronger it becomes, as it understands the wearer.

Cleansing: Salt bath method.

Naturally Occurring: Eur., N. Amer., S. Amer.

Derivation: From the Persian "lazward" - blue.

Frequency: Rare.

Bodies affected: Physical, Mental.

Continued overleaf

Lapis Lazuli (Lazurite) - con't

Birthstone Information;
Zodiac dates: November 23 - December 22.
Zodiac sign: Sagittarius, the archer.
Ruler of House: 9th.
Ruled by: Jupiter.
Associated Stones: Azurite, Lapis Lazuli.
Associated Color: Purple.
Associated Metal: Tin.
Associated Plant: Asparagus, Dandelion.
Associated Tree: Lime Oak, Birch.
Associated Country: Australia, Spain.
Associated Cities: Budapest, Cologne.
Element: Fire.
Body Area: Hips and Thighs.
Characteristics: Friendly, relaxed, outgoing, enthusiastic.

Lavender (Lavendulane)
Color: Lavender and Purple. Associated colors: Indigo.

Opens the physical body to receive spiritual enrichment. Provides feelings of joy, happiness and upliftment. When worn, aligns all the chakras of all the bodies, providing increased balance. This results in the individual becoming more creative, stronger, more loving, increasing in self mastery. When given by one and worn by the other, removes disharmony between two individuals. Lavender is one of the new age gems that it yet to "come into its own", which is fast approaching.

Types: Spheres, natural.

Wearing: Wear on crown, brow or any other chakra points for specific attention.

Healing: Crown - it can be worn for as long as comfortable for the relief of headache. Brow - for general healing, but do not restrict blood flow, snug only.

Chakra points affected: All.

Duration: Can be worn for as long as it feels comfortable - the longer worn, the stronger the effect.

Cleansing: Running water method.

Naturally Occurring: Eur., N. Amer., S. Amer.

Derivation: Named for its color.

Frequency: Rare.

Bodies affected: Physical, Emotional, Spiritual.

Lepidolite

Color: Black, brown, green, violet, clear.

Assists heart and muscle development. Balances emotional and mental bodies, producing calming, more understanding, more tolerant attitude. Dissolves hostility and depression, provides upliftment and clarity for actions taken. Provides greater insight of inner processes.

Types: Cabochons.

Wearing: Neck and heart.

Chakra points affected: Brow, neck.

Cleansing: Running water method.

Naturally Occurring: Africa, Aust., Eur., India, N. Amer., S. Amer.

Derivation: From the Greek "lepidion" - scale, and "lithos" - stone.

Frequency: Rare.

Bodies affected: Physical, Emotional, Mental.

Malachite

Color: Green, yellow. Associated colors: Green, pink, yellow.

Beneficial for the heart, teeth, glands, inflammations, and bone joint problems, including arthritic conditions. Balances emotions and opens them up, particularly for men. Breaks up blockages in all chakras, especially the heart. As a result, it soothes, calms, reduces tension and depression, aids in sub conscious understanding of events. Develops courage to make a move forward, despite unknown consequences.

Caution: 1. Should not be encased in metal (e.g. Gold, Silver). 2. Can lose it's sparkle if soaked in salt water, although running water may be used to clean. See cleansing details.

Types: Cabochons, tumble polished, natural, spheres.

Wearing: Around the neck.

Healing: Neck, and over specific area if problem known.

Chakra points affected: Neck, heart, solar plexus.

Duration: At least twenty four hours, up to a month or more.

Cleansing: Incense method.

Naturally Occurring: Africa, Eur., N. Amer.

Derivation: Historical.

Frequency: Common.

Bodies affected: Physical.

Meteorite

Color: Brown/grey.

Aids in understanding past lives, either on this or other planets. Assists in telepathic communication with extraterrestrials. Meditation is enhanced when holding or having the gem over the third eye.

Types: Tumble polished.

Wearing: Heart, neck and brow.

Naturally Occurring: Africa, Aust., Eur., India, N. Amer., S. Amer.

Chakra points affected: Brow.

Cleansing: Running water method.

Naturally Occurring: Africa, Aust., Eur., India, N. Amer., S. Amer.

Frequency: Common

Bodies affected: Mental, Spiritual

Moldavite

Color: Deep green.

Like Meteorite, Moldavite assists in communicating with extraterrestrials and understanding psychic awareness. Aids in channelling, and in balancing physical and mental bodies. Meditation is enhanced when holding or having the gem over the third area.

Types: Tumble polished.

Wearing: Heart, neck and brow.

Chakra points affected: Brow.

Cleansing: Running water method.

Naturally Occurring: Eur., India, S. Amer.

Frequency: Common

Bodies affected: Spiritual

Moonstone (Orthoclase)

Color: Clear, blue'ish, grey'ish, through to pink.

On the physical level, works with most of the centre body organs, including those of female reproduction. Assists menstrual problems, and the associated pain, stress, and anxiety. Balances emotions, providing a tolerant, sensitive, more aware attitude toward others, bringing joy and happiness. Encourages male/female viewpoint to become balanced.

Caution: Moonstone is considered to be capable of displaying both a positive and a negative influence, so care should exercised.

Types: Cabochons.

Wearing: Generally carried in pocket.

Chakra points affected: Brow, spleen, solar plexus.

Cleansing: Salt bath method.

Naturally Occurring: Africa, Aust., Eur., India, N. Amer., S. Amer.

Derivation: From the Greek "orthos" - right, and "klao" - cleave.

Frequency: Widespread.

Bodies affected: Physical, Emotional.

Birthstone Information;
Zodiac dates: June 23 - July 23.
Zodiac sign: Cancer, the crab.
Ruler of House: 4th.
Ruled by: Moon.
Associated Stones: Amber, Moonstone.
Associated Color: Grey, Green, Silver.
Associated Metal: Silver.
Associated Plant: Wild Flowering Plants.
Associated Tree: Those rich in sap.
Associated Country: NZ, Scotland.
Associated Cities: New York, Venice.
Element: Water.
Body Area: Breasts.
Characteristics: Intuitive, artistic, emotional, irrational.

Obsidian

Color: Black (Apache tears), green, blue often with red patches. Associated colors: Red.

A New Age Stone. On the physical level, assists stomach and intestines. Removes negativity and stress, disclosing ones own problems. Because of this effect, care should be exercised when using, and user must be prepared to process resultant changes. Although Obsidian is a very strong stone, it can also be a very nourishing one. Balances and connects the physical and the mental, removing mental blocks. Encourages development of latent ability. The light blue or green variety (Mt. St. Helen) develops the inner person, especially those on a spiritual journey.

Caution: 1. If negativity removed, recommended that Rose Quartz be used to "seal" individual. 2. Obsidian can awaken serious changes in the individual and should be used with discretion.

Types: Natural, tumble polished.

Wearing: Neck and base.

Healing: Over chakra point.

Chakra points affected: Neck and heart (Mt. St. H), base (A.T.).

Cleansing: Running water method.

Naturally Occurring: Africa, Aust., Eur., India, N. Amer., S. Amer.

Frequency: Common.

Bodies affected: Physical, Mental.

Onyx

Color: Black, grey, white. Associated colors: White.

Works on physical, mental and emotional aspects, balancing male/female polarities. Concentration is enhanced, aids in bringing patterns and habits to the conscious, resulting in greater self control. In so doing, draws to the required chakra, strength to break or master those habits. For those who are "up tight", or have difficulty concentrating, Onyx can be used to ground themselves.

Types: Cabochons, tumble polished, spheres.

Wearing: Quantity and size relatively unimportant. If it feels comfortable, probably is amount the individual can handle. Can be worn anywhere, but neck useful for most situations. Can be carried in pocket, as long as it is the aura.

Healing: Can be worn over base chakra if comfortable as this is area where Onyx starts to work. If individual is feeling negative or depressed, Onyx assists in highlighting the positive side of the situation.

Chakra points affected: Neck, heart, base.

Cleansing: Running water method.

Duration: Can be worn for as long as it feels comfortable. It works at the rate the individual can accept the changes that will occur.

Naturally Occurring: Eur., India, S. Amer.

Derivation: From the Greek "Onyx" - nail.

Frequency: Common.

Bodies affected: Physical, Emotional, Mental.

Opal

Color: White, pink, black, with flashes of color. Associated colors: Orange.

Differing colorants affect and cause a variety of results. In general however, glands, eyesight and lungs are strengthened. Aids in understanding the supernatural world. It calms, provides emotional balance, improves the memory, connects intuitive process to the conscious, increases level of understanding, and assists those who have trouble sleeping.

Types: Cabochons, tumble polished, spheres.

Wearing: The neck or over specific areas. It can be worn at night around the neck.

Healing: Over appropriate chakra point. Does not always provide healing on it is own, but is responsible for causing individuals to seek additional assistance when this is appropriate.

Chakra points affected: All

Duration: Wear as long as positive feelings experienced.

Cleansing: Running water method.

Naturally Occurring: Africa, Aust., Eur., India, N. Amer., S. Amer.

Derivation: From the old Indian "upala" - precious stone.

Frequency: Widespread.

Bodies affected: Physical, Mental, Spiritual.

Pearl/Mother of Pearl

Color: Pale grey lustre. Associated colors: White.

Affects the physical, mental and emotional bodies. Helpful for lung and chest disorders. Provides understanding, balance, and calming influence. Dissolves disharmonies, provides focus, protects against invasion of negative thoughts. Assists in understanding who we really are.

Caution: Pearl has both positive and negative influences, so caution is advised.

Types: Spheres.

Wearing: Around the neck affects all the chakras. When worn on specific area, concentration of that area will be highlighted.

Healing: Around the neck, or affected chakra.

Chakra points affected: Neck, heart, solar plexus.

Cleansing: Running water method.

Naturally Occurring: From the ocean: Pearl oyster, nacre, abalone.

Frequency: Common.

Bodies affected: Physical, Emotional, Mental.
Birthstone Information;
Zodiac dates: February 20 - March 21.
Zodiac sign: Pisces, the fishes.
Ruler of House: 12th.
Ruled by: Jupiter & Neptune.
Associated Stones: Amethyst, Pearl.
Associated Color: Blue Green.
Associated Metal: Tin.
Associated Plant: Water Lily.
Associated Tree: Willow, Fig, Trees near water.
Associated Country: Portugal.
Associated Cities: Seville.
Element: Water.
Body Area: Feet.
Characteristics: Emotional, intelligent, sensitive, imaginative.
Wedding anniversary gift for: Thirtieth.

Peridot (Olivine)

Color: Green or yellow. Associated colors: Yellow, green.

Assists major organs in torso, especially the blood, digestive and intestinal systems, and muscle development. Stimulates thought and intuitive processes, including personal development. Aids those suffering from insomnia. Balances mental and physical bodies, allowing a more effective role to be handled with confidence. Reduces enviousness, depression and hostility.

Types: Cabochons.

Wearing: Neck, heart, solar plexus, spleen.

Chakra points affected: Brow, heart.

Cleansing: Salt bath method.

Naturally Occurring: Africa, Eur., India, N. Amer.

Derivation: Named because of its color.

Frequency: Widespread.

Bodies affected: Physical, Mental.
Birthstone Information;
Zodiac dates: August 24 - September 23.
Zodiac sign: Virgo, the virgin.
Ruler of House: 6th.
Ruled by: Mercury.
Associated Stones: Peridot, Sapphire.
Associated Color: Navy Blue.
Associated Metal: Mercury.
Associated Plant: Small, brightly colored flowers.
Associated Tree: Nut trees.
Associated Country: Greece, Turkey.
Associated Cities: Boston, Paris.
Element: Earth.
Body Area: Bowel and Intestine.
Characteristics: Intelligent, practical, careful, orderly.

Purple Rainbow Fluorite

Color: Purple and Indigo. Associated colors: Indigo.

Assists in causing fundamental change. Enables physical body to accept greater flow of indigo ray, which influences change from a physical, materialistic view to a spiritualistic one. It brings wisdom, divinity and spiritual inspiration.

Caution: Crystalline not recommended for healing.

Types: Facets, cabochons, spheres, cylindrical, and crystalline.

Wearing: Neck and Brow Chakras. The neck chakra should be used by those people oriented towards physical and the attachments of the earth. The brow chakra should be used by those who are more spiritual and less attached to the physical.

Healing. Use on its own. Short duration and high frequency is most effective.

Chakra points affected: All

Cleansing: Salt bath method.

Duration: Wear it for as long as it feels comfortable.

Naturally occurring: Africa, Aust., Eur., India, N. Amer., S. Amer.

Frequency: Common.

Bodies affected: Physical, Spiritual.

Pyrite

Color: Pale yellow. Associated colors: Red.

Assists blood circulation, digestion, and brain activity. Produces positive outlook, removes stress, improves concentration, provides self confidence, balances emotions. Assists meditation, develops an understanding of the higher realms of the mind, opening it to growth. Spiritual growth can be further enhanced by using in conjunction with fluorite and/or amethyst.

Types: Natural, facets, cabochons.

Wearing: Neck, heart, base, solar plexus.

Chakra points affected: Crown, heart, solar plexus, base.

Cleansing: Salt bath method.

Naturally Occurring: Aust., Eur., N. Amer., S. Amer.

Derivation: From the Greek "pyr" - fire.

Frequency: Common.

Bodies affected: Physical, Emotional, Mental, Spiritual.

Quartz Crystal (clear)
Color: Clear to cloudy. Associated colors: White, violet.

Quartz is a grounding, balancing, energy centre. It benefits the pineal and pituitary glands, balances and joins the physical, emotional and mental levels. Enhances thought processes, aids meditation and thought transference, both internal and external, opens user to psychic awareness. Use provides wearer with more energy, more vitality. Clears chakra blockages. Promotes serenity, persistence, clear thinking, removes negativity. Specific crystals activate learning. Beneficial for those with eye problems or habitual headaches. A master healer, it can be used to focus it's benefits to any organ in need of repair.

Caution: Indiscriminate use of crystals over the body can cause either pulling or pushing, of positive or negative energy, into or out of the body. Therefore care is required, and should only be carried out only by those who understand what they are doing. (Use of spheres may reduce this potential problem).

Types: Natural rock crystals, facets, cabochons, spheres.

Wearing: Around the neck, or over any chakra point. Generally, the more Quartz worn, the greater the effect.

Healing: Worn around the neck, entire body balanced. Over a specific part of the body, that part is brought into balance. Over the crown for greater understanding and opening mind.

Chakra points affected: Crown, brow, neck, heart, solar plexus, spleen, base.

Duration: Spheres over any or all chakra points for about an hour, once or twice a day. Remove from top down, and ensure necklace is continually worn to continue the effect.

Quartz Crystal (clear) - con't

Cleansing: Salt bath method.

Naturally Occurring: Africa, Aust., Eur., India, N. Amer., S. Amer.

Derivation: From the Greek "Chrystalos" or "Krystalos" - clear ice.

Frequency: Widespread.

Bodies affected: Physical, Emotional, Mental.
Birthstone Information;
Zodiac dates: January 20 - February 19.
Zodiac sign: Aquarius, the water bearer.
Ruler of House: 11th.
Ruled by: Saturn & Uranus.
Associated Stones: Clear Quartz, Garnet.
Associated Color: Blue.
Associated Metal: Uranium.
Associated Plant: Orchids.
Associated Tree: Most fruit trees.
Associated Country: Sweden, Russia.
Associated Cities: Hamburg, Moscow.
Element: Air.
Body Area: Ankles.
Characteristics: Independent, open minded, serious, curious.

Rhodochrosite

Color: Light brown, orange, pink and translucent.

Affects the heart and central body organs. Resolves patterns feeding physical and emotional disharmony. It operates by destroying established patterns, cleansing, and rebuilding. Promotes self confidence, acceptance, encourages and motivates, removes depression, disharmony, and rejection. Provides foundation of emotional and physical stability. It will work regardless of individuals attitude, but enhanced by mental declaration.

Caution: 1. Faceted should only be used by experts. 2. The larger the stone, the stronger its effects.

Balancing stone: Rhodonite.

Types: Facets, cabochons, tumble polished, spheres.

Wearing: Heart and base.

Chakra points affected: Crown, heart.

Duration: From two to six months, then a few hours per day.

Cleansing: Running water method.

Naturally occurring: Eur., S. Amer.

Derivation: From the Greek "rhodon" - Rose and "chroma" - color.

Frequency: Common.

Bodies affected: Physical, Emotional.

Rhodonite

Color: Red or pink with black markings. Associated colors: Red.

Assists nervous and immune systems, reflexes and glands. Alters point of view from physical to emotional plane. Balances and grounds emotions, providing emotional well being. Increases self confidence and esteem, achievement level, compassion and understanding. For full benefit, the wearer must understand and accept changes. These fundamental changes will occur gradually.

Caution: 1. Differing colorants and markings of Rhodonite can affect the influence of the stone. 2. Do not use a stone that is too strong for you.

Types: Cabochons, tumble polished, spheres.

Wearing: Around the neck, or individual stone can be carried in the pocket.

Healing: The stronger the red or pink, the more powerful the stone.

Chakra points affected: Neck, heart.

Naturally Occurring: Africa, Eur., N. Amer., S. Amer.

Derivation: From the Greek "rhodos" - Rose colored.

Frequency: Widespread.

Bodies affected: Physical, Emotional.

Riverstone

Color: Brownish. Associated colors: Red.

Produces an increased speed of change in the body. This causes whatever change is under way to be accelerated, whether for the good or the bad. This speed of change causes other changes to manifest themselves. To be effective a conscious focus must be present. Is affected by other gemstones worn at the same time.

Caution: Accelerates changes that are in train. If diseased body, disease can accelerate speed of growth/development.

Types: Spheres.

Wearing: Around the neck.

Healing: Can be used prior to other healing to excite any area which will result in concentrated healing being given to that area.

Chakra points affected: Neck, heart.

Duration: Fifteen minutes over a given area, or for similar duration around the neck, when it assists meditation.

Cleansing: Running water method.

Naturally Occurring: Africa, Aust., Eur., India, N. Amer., S. Amer.

Frequency: Common.

Bodies affected: Physical, Emotional.

Rose Quartz

Color: Pink. Associated colors: Green, pink.

Healing, soothing crystal. Benefits circulatory system and kidneys. Balances emotional and physical bodies, including sexual organs. Aids individuals in understanding their true emotions, and repairs broken hearts. Be prepared for release of emotional energy. Reduces stress, removes apprehension, provides calming, forgiving, understanding, outlook. Vitalises imagination. The action of Rose Quartz is subtle, and helps women more than men. (Men may find Malachite more appropriate).

Caution: Do not use dyed Rose Quartz for healing.

Types: Facets, cabochons, tumble polished, spheres.

Wearing: Around the neck, the larger the more powerful.

Healing: Makes wearer aware of emotional feelings, and helps in clearing blockages. Can be used over all chakra points together to balance all the bodies, bringing physical and emotional bodies more into balance.

Chakra points affected: Heart, base.

Duration: Effects can be noticed after a few hours. Can be worn for days on end, or until wearer feels like taking it off.

Cleansing: Running water or salt bath methods.

Naturally Occurring: Africa, Eur., N. Amer., S. Amer.

Derivation: Named after its color.

Frequency: Widespread.

Bodies affected: Physical, Emotional.

Rubellite

Color: Rose, pale red. Associated colors: Red.

On the physical level, Rubellite has special powers in assisting blood disorders and diseases, including anaemia. Other major organs that benefit from the gentle, soothing strength include the liver, kidneys, and brain. Emotionally, fear and negativity are reduced, and acceptance of the situation is enhanced. On the spiritual level, encourages growth, and the third eye (brow) can be opened to allow better understanding of the supernatural.

Types: Natural, facets, cabochons.

Wearing: As jewellery, (ring, necklace), or carried in pocket.

Chakra points affected: Brow, neck, heart.

Cleansing: Initially salt water method. Provided it is used as a one person stone, subsequent cleansings can be running water method.

Naturally Occurring: Africa, Eur., N. Amer., S. Amer.

Derivation: From the Latin "rubellus" - reddish.

Frequency: Rare.

Bodies affected: Physical, Spiritual

Ruby

Color: Red. Associated colors: Red.

Ray carried: Red.

Very powerful stone. Provides energy to the whole body, especially the heart, circulation, immune, and blood systems. Develops concentration, which can assist in quarrelsome situations. Expands original thinking, and in life threatening situations, amplifies desire to live. Ruby teaches the force of love, providing a direct link between the emotions and the physical body. Brings the emotions to a physical level. (Sapphire brings the mental level to the physical level).

Caution: 1. Use crystal variety with care. 2. Many present day rubies are artificial, which are ineffective.

Types: Natural, facets, cabochons, spheres.

Wearing: Wear anywhere that is comfortable, but principally affects the heart and lower chakras.

Healing: Ruby works on the emotions, and brings to the conscious awareness the reasons for distress between the emotional and physical. It is then up to the individual to do something about it. Ruby works whether you believe it or not, or want it to or not. It will also give powerful love. This love is needed to accept the required changes.

Chakra points affected: All.

Duration: Starts to work immediately. Wear if it feels comfortable, but start using for short duration's, extending gradually.

Cleansing: Salt bath method.

Naturally Occurring: Africa, Aust., Eur., India, N. Amer.

Associated stone: Sapphire.

Derivation: From the Latin "rubeus" - red.

Frequency: Rare.

Continued overleaf

Ruby - con't

Bodies affected: Physical, Emotional.

Birthstone Information;
Zodiac dates: March 22 - April 20.
Zodiac sign: Aries, the ram
Ruler of House: 1st.
Ruled by: Mars.
Associated Stones: Diamond, Ruby.
Associated Color: Red.
Associated Color: Red.
Associated Metal: Copper.
Associated Plant: Geranium, Honeysuckle, Thistle.
Associated Tree: All thorn bearing trees.
Associated Country: England, France.
Associated Cities: Florence, Naples.
Element: Fire.
Body Area: Head.
Characteristics: Bold, determined, impatient, energetic.

Wedding anniversary gift for: fortieth.

Rutilated Quartz (Rutile)

Color: White, brown, green

Stimulates brain activity, strengthens immune and respiratory system, eases depression by warding off negative vibes. Provides self confidence, peace of mind, connection with higher self and aids in mental communication. Brings unconscious habits to the fore, allowing a conscious decision to be made regarding control. When used with other healing stones, results can be accelerated. (Rutilated Quartz is rutile within Quartz and combines the effects of both).

Types: Cabochons, tumble polished.

Chakra points affected: Brow, neck, heart.

Cleansing: Salt bath method.

Naturally Occurring: Africa, Aust., Eur., India, N. Amer., S. Amer.

Frequency: Widespread.

Bodies affected: Physical, Mental.

Sapphire

Color: Blue and dark blue. Also comes in green, yellow, pinkish and orange (Padparadjah). Associated colors: Blue.

Rays carried: Blue and indigo.

Varying colors of sapphire strengthen the heart, kidneys, glands, eyes and ears. Sapphire nourishes and balances the mind, bringing wisdom, happiness and peace to the fore. Thinking becomes clearer, confusion disappears, memory improves. Helps development on the spiritual level. Puts thoughts in order and perspective. Teaches discrimination, promotes self control reducing craving for unhelpful habits. (Sapphire brings the mental to the physical level, whilst Ruby brings the emotions to the physical level).

Caution: Sapphire affects some people by subduing emotions, and focussing on worldly aspects. In this case, use should be discontinued.

Types: Natural, facets, cabochons, tumble polished, spheres.

Wearing: Neck, brow, fingers.

Healing: Sapphire can be worn around the neck in a short strand. Eyesight and hearing will improve.

Chakra points affected: Brow - dark blue and black, neck - lighter blues and pinks.

Duration: Sapphire can be worn constantly. Remove if it feels uncomfortable.

Cleansing: Salt bath method.

Naturally Occurring: Africa, Aust., Eur., India, N. Amer.

Associated stone: Ruby.

Derivation: Unknown.

Frequency: Rare.

Sapphire - con't

Bodies affected: Physical, Mental.

Birthstone Information;
Zodiac dates: August 24 - September 23.
Zodiac sign: Virgo, the virgin.
Ruler of House: 6th.
Ruled by: Mercury.
Associated Stones: Peridot, Sapphire.
Associated Color: Navy Blue.
Associated Metal: Mercury.
Associated Plant: Small, brightly colored flowers.
Associated Tree: Nut trees.
Associated Country: Greece, Turkey.
Associated Cities: Boston, Paris.
Element: Earth.
Body Area: Bowel and Intestine.
Characteristics: Intelligent, practical, careful, orderly.

Wedding anniversary gift for: Forty-fifth.

Sardonyx (Sard & Onyx layers)

Color: Tan, golden, red.

On the emotional level, Sardonyx is credited with easing depression, enhancing self control, self confidence and providing upliftment. Humility, inner strength and ability to grieve are all enhanced. Reportedly draws good luck to the wearer.

Types: Cabochons.

Chakra points affected: Neck.

Cleansing: Incense method.

Naturally Occurring: Eur, India, S. Amer.

Derivation: From "Sardis", Greek city used for transiting Sardonyx.

Frequency: Rare.

Bodies affected: Emotional.

Silver

Color: Silver white. Associated colors: White.

Enhances circulation, heart, blood, and glandular systems, and problems with ENT (ear, nose & throat) ailments. Cleanses the body, and assists sexual and urinary organs. Assists mental processes, and provides balancing between emotional and physical planes.

Caution: An over abundance of silver being absorbed into the body can lead to physical ailments. Do not wear without giving body a break now and then.

Wearing: Anywhere.

Cleansing: Incense method, then use a commercial cleaner.

Naturally Occurring: Africa, Aust., Eur., India, N. Amer., S. Amer.

Derivation: Historical.

Frequency: Widespread.

Wedding anniversary gift for: Twenty-fifth.

Smoky Quartz

Color: Brown (from very light to very dark). Associated colors: Red.

Aids the centre body organs, including bowel, rectal and sexual organs. Provides balancing between physical and mental levels. Removes negativity, depression, assists in facing reality. Enhances intuition and interpretation of feelings. Increases self-respect in oneself. Aids meditation, dream memory, interpretation and understanding.

Caution: Do not use irradiated crystals, which will cause disharmony, affecting mental and emotional points of view. (Crystals artificially irradiated can be healed by experienced practitioners).

Types: Facets, cabochons, tumble polished.

Wearing: Solar plexus, base, spleen.

Chakra points affected: Neck, solar plexus, base.

Cleansing: Salt bath method.

Naturally Occurring: Africa, Aust., Eur., India, N. Amer., S. Amer.

Derivation: Named for its color.

Frequency: Rare.

Bodies affected: Physical, Mental.

Birthstone Information;
Zodiac dates: December 23 - January 19.
Zodiac sign: Capricorn, the goat.
Ruler of House: 10th.
Ruled by: Saturn.
Associated Stones: Agate (Fire), Smoky Quartz.
Associated Color: Brown, Black.
Associated Metal: Lead.
Associated Plant: Ivy, Pansies.
Associated Tree: Pine, Elm, Poplar.
Associated Country: India, Mexico.
Associated Cities: Delhi, Oxford.
Element: Earth.
Body Area: Knees.
Characteristics: Ambitious, cautious, patient, persistent.

Sodalite

Color: Soft blue, deep blue, white, green. Associated colors: Indigo, blue.

Strengthens metabolism, lymphatic, pancreas, and endocrine systems, pineal and pituitary glands. Balances the mental body, removing fear, replacing with clarity of mind, logical thinking, and truth. Assists in acceptance of this truth. Provides enthusiasm and happiness in attitude to life. Increases spiritual awareness, providing increased understanding and broader outlook.

Types: Cabochons, tumble polished.

Healing: Over crown, brow or neck.

Chakra points affected: Brow, neck.

Cleansing: Running water method.

Naturally Occurring: Africa, Eur., N. Amer., S. Amer.

Derivation: Named after its chemical composition.

Frequency: Rare.

Bodies affected: Physical, Mental.

Sugilite

Color: Purplish.

Aids glandular system, especially the pineal and pituitary glands, the heart, purifying the body. Advances spiritual awareness bringing recognition of higher spiritual order. Develops an understanding of the relationship between the intuitive and logical levels. Balances emotions.

Wearing: Brow, neck.

Chakra points affected: Crown, brow.

Cleansing: Salt bath method.

Naturally Occurring: Africa, Aust., Eur., India, N. Amer., S. Amer.

Frequency: Common.

Bodies affected: Physical, Mental, Spiritual.

Tiger's eye

Color: Brown, streaked with yellow.

Develops and strengthens centre body organs, concentration and perception. Balances and connects emotional and mental bodies, resulting in more relaxed, more understanding and tolerant outlook, and enhances self confidence of the wearer. Brings unconscious thought patterns into focus where they can be analysed. Develops alternative attitudes and perceptions. Brings good luck.

Types: Facets, cabochons, tumble polished.

Wearing: Spleen, solar plexus.

Chakra points affected: Solar Plexus.

Cleansing: Salt bath method.

Naturally Occurring: Aust., N. Amer., S. Amer.

Derivation: After its color and appearance.

Frequency: Common.

Bodies affected: Physical, Emotional.

Topaz

Color: Yellow to brown. White and blue are common, but not gem quality. Associated colors: Yellow, orange.

Aids lungs and nervous system, detoxifies body, assists throat aliments. Calms and instructs those experiencing sleeplessness. Balances emotions, reduces stress, providing peaceful, harmonious, relaxed outlook. Assists in understanding strengths and where to apply for best return. Aids in developing character and confidence in oneself. Develops contact with higher self, and with psychic perceptions. Assists in controlling undesirable habits.

Types: Natural, facets, cabochons.

Wearing: Neck, spleen, carried in pocket.

Chakra points affected: Crown & heart - yellow, solar plexus - brown.

Cleansing: Running water method.

Naturally Occurring: Africa, Eur., N. Amer., S. Amer.

Derivation: After the Topasos island in Red sea.

Frequency: Rare.

Bodies affected: Physical, Emotional, Mental.
Birthstone Information;
Zodiac dates: April 21 - March 21.
Zodiac sign: Taurus, the bull.
Ruler of House: 2nd.
Ruled by: Venus.
Associated Stones: Carnelian, Topaz.
Associated Color: Pink, Pale Blue.
Associated Metal: Copper.
Associated Plant: Rose, Poppy - Violet.
Associated Tree: Ash/Cypress, Apple.
Associated Country: Ireland, Switzerland.
Associated Cities: Dublin, Lucerne.
Element: Earth.
Body Area: Throat.
Characteristics: Loving, loyal, possessive, stubborn.

Tourmaline (all colors)
See also: Indicolite (blue, blue/green), Rubellite (pink, red).

Color: Pink/green (watermelon), black (schorl), brown (dravite). Associated colors: Green, pink.

Master healing stone. Generally beneficial for glands, nerves, and for reducing negativity of most types. (Differing inclusions emphasise different influences). With green inclusions, provides body, brain, and mind vitality, dissipating apprehension, aids mental disorders, strengthens endocrine system. Watermelon balances male/female polarities, and has protective qualities. Black and brown tourmaline improve communication with others, enhances tolerance, self confidence, and provide grounding. Meditation and channelling can be enhanced by gems that have been activated for the purpose.

Types: Natural, facets, cabochons, crystals.

Wearing: Depends on color.

Healing: Placed near heart, enhances understanding and balances male vs female outlook. At the crown it removes pain, improves self worth. At the brow, channelling is enhanced if individual is ready for such activity.

Chakra points affected: Heart - especially green and pink.

Cleansing: Salt bath method.

Naturally Occurring: Africa, Aust., Eur., India, N. Amer., S. Amer.

Derivation: Historical.

Frequency: Common.

Bodies affected: Physical, Mental, Spiritual.

Continued overleaf

Tourmaline (all colors) - con't

Birthstone Information;
Zodiac dates: May 22 - June 22.
Zodiac sign: Gemini, the twins.
Ruler of House: 3rd.
Ruled by: Mercury.
Associated Stones: Aquamarine, Tourmaline.
Associated Color: Yellow.
Associated Metal: Mercury.
Associated Plant: Lily of the Valley, Lavender.
Associated Tree: Nut Trees.
Associated Country: USA, Wales.
Associated Cities: London, Melbourne.
Element: Air.
Body Area: Chest, arms and hands.
Characteristics: Clever, curious, expressive, indecisive.

Wedding anniversary gift for: Forty-fifth.

Turquoise

Color: Light blue, sky blue, green. Associated colors: Blue

Assists entire body, strengthening circulatory, respiratory, and nervous systems, throat, lungs, eyes, and blood. Balances emotions, provides peace of mind, provides courage, (especially for public presentations), enhances meditation. Increases consideration and humanity to others. Useful stone in protecting carrier from evil forces.

Caution: There are reconstructed Turquoise gems on the market, which do not provide the same beneficial results.

Types: Cabochons, natural stones, tumble polished.

Wearing: Neck, brow.
Healing: Can be carried or worn around the neck which affects all of the body.

Chakra points affected: Neck, heart.

Cleansing: Running water method but don't place in direct sun.

Naturally Occurring: Eur., India

Derivation: Means Turkish stone.

Frequency: Rare.

Bodies affected: Physical, Emotional.
Birthstone Information;
Zodiac dates: October 24 - November 22.
Zodiac sign: Scorpio, the scorpion.
Ruler of House: 8th.
Ruled by: Mars & Pluto.
Associated Stones: Aventurine, Turquoise.
Associated Color: Green.
Associated Metal: Iron.
Associated Plant: Those with dark red flowers, eg Rhododendron.
Associated Tree: Bushy trees, blackthorn.
Associated Country: Norway, Syria.
Associated Cities: Liverpool, Washington, DC.
Element: Water.
Body Area: Sexual Organs.
Characteristics: Aggressive, moody, secretive, leadership.
Wedding anniversary gift for: Fifty-fifth.

Variscite

Color: White, green.

Strengthens heart, nervous and blood systems. Balances physical and mental bodies, providing calm, relaxed, outlook.

Types: Cabochons.

Wearing: Heart, neck.

Chakra points affected: Neck.

Cleansing: Salt bath method.

Naturally Occurring: Aust, Eur., N. Amer., S. Amer.

Derivation: Historical.

Frequency: Rare.

Bodies affected: Physical, Mental.

Zircon (Hyacinth)
Color: Yellow, brown, red. Associated colors: White, violet.

Aids bowel problems, balances glandular system, strengthens the mind, assists brain disorders. Balances emotional outlook, improving self worth, and removes scepticism of others. Aids those having trouble sleeping, especially if induced by emotional or mental problems.

Types: Facets, cabochons.

Wearing: Neck, base.

Chakra points affected: Crown, neck, base.

Cleansing: Salt bath method but don't place in the sun.

Naturally Occurring: Africa, Aust., Eur., N. Amer., S. Amer.

Frequency: Common.

Bodies affected: Physical, Emotional.

Birthstone Information;
Zodiac dates: July 24 - August 23.
Zodiac sign: Leo, the lion.
Ruler of House: 5th.
Ruled by: Sun.
Associated Color: Orange, Gold.
Associated Stones: Jasper, Ruby.
Associated Metal: Gold.
Associated Plant: Sunflower, Marigold, Rosemary.
Associated Tree: Orange & all citrus trees, Bay and Palm.
Associated Country: Italy, Rumania.
Associated Cities: Los Angeles, Rome.
Element: Fire.
Body Area: Heart and Spine.
Characteristics: Powerful, proud, energetic, strong-willed.

There is a huge resource available

to us just waiting to be utilised

4. Cross Reference for Gem Names

This list contains minerals that are sometimes known under multiple names. It also includes minerals where a substantial similarity to another exists, although it is not necessarily 100% identical. It will depend on why you are looking for a specific mineral as to whether the similar mineral is appropriate. If in doubt, ask your supplier.

Agate - chapter 3.
Albite - see future releases of this book/disk.
Alexandrite - see future releases of this book/disk.
Almadine - see Garnet
Amazonite - chapter 3.
Amber - chapter 3.
Amethyst - chapter 3.
Ametrine - see Amethyst and/or Citrine
Angelite - see future releases of this book/disk.
Anhydrite - see future releases of this book/disk.
Apatite - see future releases of this book/disk.
Apophylite - see future releases of this book/disk.
Aquamarine - chapter 3.
Aragonite - see future releases of this book/disk.
Asteria - see future releases of this book/disk.
Atacamite - see future releases of this book/disk.
Aventurine - chapter 3.
Azurite - chapter 3.
Azuremalachite - see future releases of this book/disk.
Azuremalachite - see separate entries Azurite and/or
                              Malachite.
Barite - see future releases of this book/disk.
Benitoite - see future releases of this book/disk.
Beryllonite - see future releases of this book/disk.
Biotite - see Lepidolite
Bloodstone - chapter 3.
Blue John - see Fluorite

Blue Lace Agate - see Agate
Blue Quartz - see future releases of this book/disk.
Blue Tourmaline - see Indicolite
Boji Stone - see future releases of this book/disk.
Bornite - see future releases of this book/disk.
Bowenite - see future releases of this book/disk.
Cairngorm - see Smoky Quartz
Calcite - chapter 3.
Carbuncle - see Garnet
Carnelian - chapter 3.
Cassiterite - chapter 3.
Cat's Eye - see future releases of this book/disk.
Celestite - chapter 3.
Cerussite - see future releases of this book/disk.
Chalcedony - chapter 3.
Chalcopyrite - see future releases of this book/disk.
Charoite - see future releases of this book/disk.
Chiastolite - see future releases of this book/disk.
Chrysoberyl - chapter 3.
Chrysocolla - chapter 3.
Chrysolite - see Peridot (Olivine)
Chrysoprase - chapter 3.
Cinnabar - see Mercury
Citrine - chapter 3.
Clear Quartz - see Quartz
Copper - chapter 3.
Coral - chapter 3.
Corundum - chapter 3.
Cowrie - see future releases of this book/disk.
Creedite - see future releases of this book/disk.
Crocoite - see future releases of this book/disk.
Cross Stone - see Chiastolite
Crystal - see Quartz
Cuprite - see future releases of this book/disk.
Cymophane - see Cat's Eye
Danburite - see future releases of this book/disk.

Desert Rose - see Barite
Diamond - chapter 3.
Diopside - see future releases of this book/disk.
Dioptase - chapter 3.
Double Terminated Quartz - see Quartz
Dravite - see Tourmaline
Durangite - see future releases of this book/disk.
Eilat Stone - see future releases of this book/disk.
Elbaite - see Tourmaline
Emerald - chapter 3.
Enstatite - see future releases of this book/disk.
Epidote - see future releases of this book/disk.
Erythrite - see future releases of this book/disk.
Fairy Cross - see Staurolite
Feather Rock - see Jamesonite
Feldspar - chapter 3.
Fire Agate - see Agate
Flint - see future releases of this book/disk.
Floating Stone - see Pumice
Fluorite - chapter 3.
Galena - see Lead
Garnet - chapter 3.
Gem Silica - see future releases of this book/disk.
Gold - chapter 3.
Gold Topaz - see future releases of this book/disk.
Golden Beryl - see Heliodor
Graphite - see future releases of this book/disk.
Grass Stone - see Rutillated Quartz
Haematite - chapter 3.
Haite - see future releases of this book/disk.
Hanksite - see future releases of this book/disk.
Hawk's eye - see future releases of this book/disk.
Heliodore - chapter 3.
Heliotrope - see Bloodstone
Hematite - see Haematite
Herderite - see future releases of this book/disk.

Herkimer Diamond - see future releases of this book/disk.
Hiddenite - see Green Kunzite
Howlite - see future releases of this book/disk.
Hyacinth - see Zircon
Iceland Spar - see Calcite
Imperial Topaz - see Gold Topaz
Inca Rose - see Rhodochrosite
Indicolite - chapter 3.
Indigo - see Indicolite
Iolite - see future releases of this book/disk.
Ivorite - chapter 3.
Ivory - see Ivorite
Jacinth - see Zircon
Jadeite - see Jade
Jade - chapter 3.
Jamesonite - see future releases of this book/disk.
Jasper - chapter 3.
Jet - see future releases of this book/disk.
Kunzite - chapter 3.
Kyanite - chapter 3.
Labradorite - see future releases of this book/disk.
Lapis Lazuli - chapter 3.
Larimar - see future releases of this book/disk.
Lavender - chapter 3.
Lavendulane - see Lavender
Lazulite - see future releases of this book/disk.
Lazurite - see future releases of this book/disk.
Lead - see future releases of this book/disk.
Leopard skin Jasper - see Jasper
Lepidolite - chapter 3.
Loadstone - see Lodestone
Lodestone - see future releases of this book/disk.
Magnesium - see future releases of this book/disk.
Magnetite - see Lodestone
Malachite - chapter 3.
Marble - see future releases of this book/disk.

Marcasite - see future releases of this book/disk.
Meerschaum - see Sepiolite
Meteorite - chapter 3.
Mica - see Lepidolite
Moldavite - chapter 3.
Moonstone - chapter 3.
Morganite - see future releases of this book/disk.
Morion - see Smoky Quartz
Muscovite - see Lepidolite
Moss Agate - see Agate
Mother of Pearl - see Pearl
Nephrite - see Jade
Obsidian - chapter 3.
Olivine - see Peridot
Onyx - chapter 3.
Opal - chapter 3.
Orpiment - see Realgar
Orthoclase - see Moonstone
Pad - short for Padparadjah
Padparadjah - see Sapphire
Peacock Ore - see future releases of this book/disk.
Pearl - chapter 3.
Peridot - chapter 3.
Petrified Wood - see future releases of this book/disk.
Phlogopite - see Lepidolite
Pink Carnelian - see Carnelian
Pink Spodumene - see Kunzite
Pink Tourmaline - see Elbaite
Plancheite - see future releases of this book/disk.
Platinum - see future releases of this book/disk.
Poppy Jasper - see Jasper
Prase - see future releases of this book/disk.
Pumice - see future releases of this book/disk.
Purple Rainbow Fluorite - chapter 3.
Pyrite - chapter 3.
Pyrope - see Garnet

Quartz - chapter 3.
Quicksilver - see Mercury
Realgar - see future releases of this book/disk.
Red Coral - see Coral
Red Garnet - see Garnet
Red Quartz - see future releases of this book/disk.
Red Spinel - see Spinel
Red Tourmaline - see Tourmaline
Rhodochrosite - chapter 3.
Rhodolite - see Garnet
Rhodonite - chapter 3.
Rhyolite - see future releases of this book/disk.
Riverstone - chapter 3.
Rock Crystal - see Quartz
Rose Quartz - chapter 3.
Roselle - see Rose Quartz
Royal Azel - see Sugilite
Rubellite - chapter 3.
Ruby - chapter 3.
Rutilated Quartz - chapter 3.
Rutile - see Rutillated Quartz
Salt - see Haite
Sandstone - see future releases of this book/disk.
Sapphire - chapter 3.
Sard - see future releases of this book/disk.
Sardonyx - chapter 3.
Scapolite - see future releases of this book/disk.
Scarab - see future releases of this book/disk.
Schorl - see Tourmaline
Selenite - see future releases of this book/disk.
Sepiolite - see future releases of this book/disk.
Serpentina - see future releases of this book/disk.
Serpentine - see future releases of this book/disk.
Shattuckite - see future releases of this book/disk.
Silex - see Jasper
Silver - chapter 3.

Smithsonite - see future releases of this book/disk.
Smoky Quartz - chapter 3.
Snakeskin Agate - see Agate
Soapstone - see future releases of this book/disk.
Sodalite - chapter 3.
Spessartin - see Garnet.
Sphene - see future releases of this book/disk.
Spinel - see future releases of this book/disk.
Spodumene - see Kunzite.
Star Sapphire - see future releases of this book/disk.
Staurolite - see future releases of this book/disk.
Strawberry Quartz - see future releases of this book/disk.
Succinite - see Amber
Sugalite - see Sugilite.
Sugilite - chapter 3
Sunstone - see Aventurine
Taconite - see Haematite
Tektite - see Meteorite
Tiger's Eye - chapter 3.
Topaz - chapter 3.
Tourmaline - chapter 3.
Tsavorite - see Garnet
Turquoise - chapter 3.
Uvarovite - see Garnet
Variscite - chapter 3.
Watermelon - see Watermelon Tourmaline
Watermelon Tourmaline - see Tourmaline
Wonderstone - see Rhyolite
Zircon - chapter 3.
Zoisite - see future releases of this book/disk.

5. The Zodiac

Zodiac dates: March 22 - April 20.
Zodiac sign: Aries, the ram. ♈
Ruler of House: 1st.
Ruled by: Mars.
Associated Stones: Diamond, Ruby.
Associated Color: Red.
Associated Metal: Copper.
Associated Plant: Geranium, Honeysuckle, Thistle.
Associated Tree: All thorn bearing trees.
Associated Country: England, France.
Associated Cities: Florence, Naples.
Element: Fire.
Body Area: Head.
Characteristics: Bold, determined, impatient, energetic.

Zodiac dates: April 21 - May 21.
Zodiac sign: Taurus, the bull. ♉
Ruler of House: 2nd.
Ruled by: Venus.
Associated Stones: Carnelian, Topaz.
Associated Color: Pink, Pale Blue.
Associated Metal: Copper.
Associated Plant: Rose, Poppy - Violet.
Associated Tree: Ash/Cypress, Apple.
Associated Country: Ireland, Switzerland.
Associated Cities: Dublin, Lucerne.
Element: Earth.
Body Area: Throat.
Characteristics: Loving, loyal, possessive, stubborn.

The Zodiac - Con't

Zodiac dates: May 22 - June 22.
Zodiac sign: Gemini, the twins. ♊
Ruler of House: 3rd.
Ruled by: Mercury.
Associated Stones: Aquamarine, Tourmaline.
Associated Color: Yellow.
Associated Metal: Mercury.
Associated Plant: Lily of the Valley, Lavender.
Associated Tree: Nut Trees.
Associated Country: USA, Wales.
Associated Cities: London, Melbourne.
Element: Air.
Body Area: Chest, arms and hands.
Characteristics: Clever, curious, expressive, indecisive.

Zodiac dates: June 23 - July 23.
Zodiac sign: Cancer, the crab. ♋
Ruler of House: 4th.
Ruled by: Moon.
Associated Stones: Amber, Moonstone.
Associated Color: Grey, Green, Silver.
Associated Metal: Silver.
Associated Plant: Wild Flowering Plants.
Associated Tree: Those rich in sap.
Associated Country: NZ, Scotland.
Associated Cities: New York, Venice.
Element: Water.
Body Area: Breasts.
Characteristics: Intuitive, artistic, emotional, irrational.

The Zodiac - Con't

Zodiac dates: July 24 - August 23.
Zodiac sign: Leo, the lion. ♌
Ruler of House: 5th.
Ruled by: Sun.
Associated Color: Orange, Gold.
Associated Stones: Jasper, Ruby.
Associated Metal: Gold.
Associated Plant: Sunflower, Marigold, Rosemary.
Associated Tree: Orange & all citrus trees, Bay and Palm.
Associated Country: Italy, Rumania.
Associated Cities: Los Angeles, Rome.
Element: Fire.
Body Area: Heart and Spine.
Characteristics: Powerful, proud, energetic, strong-willed.

Zodiac dates: August 24 - September 23.
Zodiac sign: Virgo, the virgin. ♍
Ruler of House: 6th.
Ruled by: Mercury.
Associated Stones: Peridot, Sapphire.
Associated Color: Navy Blue.
Associated Metal: Mercury.
Associated Plant: Small, brightly colored flowers.
Associated Tree: Nut trees.
Associated Country: Greece, Turkey.
Associated Cities: Boston, Paris.
Element: Earth.
Body Area: Bowel and Intestine.
Characteristics: Intelligent, practical, careful, orderly.

The Zodiac - Con't

Zodiac dates: September 24 - October 23.
Zodiac sign: Libra, the scales. ♎
Ruler of House: 7th.
Ruled by: Venus.
Associated Stones: Emerald, Padparadjah.
Associated Color: Pink, Blue.
Associated Metal: Copper.
Associated Plant: All with Blue flowers, Large roses.
Associated Tree: Ash.
Associated Country: Austria, Japan.
Associated Cities: Lisbon, Vienna.
Element: Air.
Body Area: Kidneys.
Characteristics: Loving, intelligent, pleasant, thoughtful.

Zodiac dates: October 24 - November 22.
Zodiac sign: Scorpio, the scorpion. ♏
Ruler of House: 8th.
Ruled by: Mars & Pluto.
Associated Stones: Aventurine, Turquoise.
Associated Color: Green.
Associated Metal: Iron.
Associated Plant: Those with dark red flowers, eg
Rhododendron.
Associated Tree: Bushy trees, blackthorn.
Associated Country: Norway, Syria.
Associated Cities: Liverpool, Washington, DC.
Element: Water.
Body Area: Sexual Organs.
Characteristics: Aggressive, moody, secretive, leadership.

The Zodiac - Con't

Zodiac dates: November 23 - December 22.
Zodiac sign: Sagittarius, the archer. ♐
Ruler of House: 9th.
Ruled by: Jupiter.
Associated Stones: Azurite, Lapis Lazuli.
Associated Color: Purple.
Associated Metal: Tin.
Associated Plant: Asparagus, Dandelion.
Associated Tree: Lime Oak, Birch.
Associated Country: Australia, Spain.
Associated Cities: Budapest, Cologne.
Element: Fire.
Body Area: Hips and Thighs.
Characteristics: Friendly, relaxed, outgoing, enthusiastic.

Zodiac dates: December 23 - January 19.
Zodiac sign: Capricorn, the goat. ♑
Ruler of House: 10th.
Ruled by: Saturn.
Associated Stones: Agate (Fire), Smoky Quartz.
Associated Color: Brown, Black.
Associated Metal: Lead.
Associated Plant: Ivy, Pansies.
Associated Tree: Pine, Elm, Poplar.
Associated Country: India, Mexico.
Associated Cities: Delhi, Oxford.
Element: Earth.
Body Area: Knees.
Characteristics: Ambitious, cautious, patient, persistent.

The Zodiac - Con't

Zodiac dates: January 20 - February 19.
Zodiac sign: Aquarius, the water bearer. ♒
Ruler of House: 11th.
Ruled by: Saturn & Uranus.
Associated Stones: Clear Quartz, Garnet.
Associated Color: Blue.
Associated Metal: Uranium.
Associated Plant: Orchids.
Associated Tree: Most fruit trees.
Associated Country: Sweden, Russia.
Associated Cities: Hamburg, Moscow.
Element: Air.
Body Area: Ankles.
Characteristics: Independent, open minded, serious, curious.

Zodiac dates: February 20 - March 21.
Zodiac sign: Pisces, the fishes. ♓
Ruler of House: 12th.
Ruled by: Jupiter & Neptune.
Associated Stones: Amethyst, Pearl.
Associated Color: Blue Green.
Associated Metal: Tin.
Associated Plant: Water Lily.
Associated Tree: Willow, Fig, Trees near water.
Associated Country: Portugal.
Associated Cities: Seville.
Element: Water.
Body Area: Feet.
Characteristics: Emotional, intelligent, sensitive, imaginative.

We cannot be here (on earth) just to earn money to live, experience life, procreate and then die. There MUST be more to it than that

6. Gemstones and Associations with Physical Ailments

Abrasions	Agate
	Amazonite
	Copper
	Haematite
	Rhodochrosite
	Rubellite
	Sodalite
Acceptance	Agate
	Amazonite
	Cassiterite
Acidity	Bismuth
	Dolomite
	Peridot
Adrenal Glands	Chrysoberyl
Aggression (moderation of)	Bloodstone
	Chrysoberyl
Alcoholism	Amethyst
Anaemia	Bloodstone
	Citrine
	Rubellite
Anger	Amethyst
	Carnelian
	Indicolite
Angina	Dioptase
Anus	Smoky Quartz

Anxiety	Azurite
	Lapis Lazuli
	Moonstone
Arthritis	Copper
	Malachite
Asthma	Amber
	Jade
Astral Projection	Double Terminated
	Quartz Crystal
Aura	Coral
	Diamond
	Heliodore
	Indicolite
	Onyx
Bad Temper	Emerald
	Bloodstone
Balance	Amber
	Aquamarine
	Aventurine
	Bloodstone
	Coral
	Chrysoprase
	Fluorite
	Haematite
	Jade
	Kunzite
	Malachite
	Moonstone
	Pearl
	Pyrite

Balance - Con't	Quartz Crystal
	Rhodonite
	Rose Quartz
	Sodalite
	Sugalite
	Tiger's Eye
	Topaz
	Tourmaline
	Turquoise
Bleeding	Bloodstone
Blood	Amethyst
	Aventurine
	Bloodstone
	Carnelian
	Cassiterite
	Citrine
	Copper
	Fluorite
	Garnet
	Haematite
	Heliodore
	Jade
	Jasper
	Kunzite
	Peridot
	Rubellite
	Ruby
	Turquoise
	Variscite
Blood Circulation	Amethyst
	Bloodstone
	Citrine
	Copper

Blood Circulation - Con't	Pyrite
	Ruby
	Turquoise
Blood Clots	Amethyst
	Bloodstone
	Haematite
Blood Pressure (high)	Dioptase
	Jade/Jadeite
Blood Pressure (low)	Garnet
	Ruby
Bone Joints	Malachite
Bones	Calcite
	Cassiterite
	Chrysocolla
	Coral
	Emerald
	Fluorite
	Garnet
	Pearl
Bowel	Smoky Quartz
	Zircon
Brain	Diamond
	Emerald
	Green Tourmaline
	Jasper
	Lapis Lazuli
	Pyrite
	Rubellite
	Rutilated Quartz
	Zircon

Broken Heart	Rose Quartz
Bronchitis	Amber
Calcification	Calcite Garnet Pearl
Calming	Amber Amethyst Aquamarine Aventurine Carnelian Chrysoprase Heliodore Jadeite Kunzite Lepidolite Malachite Opal Pearl Rose Quartz Topaz Variscite
Cancer	Amethyst Rose Quartz Smoky Quartz Magnetite
Chakra Opening	Citrine
Channelling	Amethyst
Chest	Amber Pearl

Circulation	Amethyst
	Bloodstone
	Citrine
	Copper
	Pyrite
	Ruby
	Turquoise
Clarity	Aquamarine
	Carnelian
	Indicolite
	Lapis Lazuli
	Sapphire
	Sodalite
	Quartz Crystal
Colon	Citrine
Concentration	Carnelian
	Fluorite
	Onyx
	Pyrite
	Ruby
	Tiger's Eye
Courage	Agate
	Haematite
Creativity	Amazonite
	Aquamarine
	Aventurine
	Bloodstone
	Celestite
	Coral
	Fluorite
	Garnet

Creativity - Con't	Kyanite
	Lavender
Cuts & Bruises	See Abrasions
Death	Amazonite
	Aquamarine
	Chrysocolla
	Citrine
Depression	Amber
	Aventurine
	Garnet
	Lapis Lazuli
	Lepidolite
	Malachite
	Peridot
	Rhodochrosite
	Rutilated Quartz
	Sardonyx
	Smoky Quartz
Despair	Heliodore
	Rhodochrosite
Detoxification	Carnelian
	Copper
	Garnet
	Topaz
Diabetes	Jade
Digestion	Carnelian
	Coral
	Peridot
	Pyrite

Disharmony	Carnelian
Dreams	Indicolite
	Jade
	Smoky Quartz
Ear Trouble	Sapphire
	Silver
Emotional Insecurity and/or Inflexibility	Amber
	Aventurine
	Carnelian
	Chrysoprase
	Emerald
	Haematite
	Malachite
	Moonstone
	Jadeite
	Jasper
	Onyx
	Rhodonite
	Rhodochrosite
Endocrine System	Sodalite
	Tourmaline
Energy	Haematite
Envy	Carnelian
Eyesight	Aquamarine
	Emerald
	Jadeite
	Kunzite
	Opal
	Quartz Crystal

Eyesight- Con't	Sapphire
	Turquoise
Forgiveness	Chrysoberyl
	Rose Quartz
Glands	Aquamarine
	Jasper
	Malachite
	Opal
	Rhodonite
	Sapphire
	Silver
	Sugalite
	Tourmaline
	Zircon
Good Luck	Dioptase
	Sardonyx
	Tiger's Eye
Grief	Chrysocolla
	Sardonyx
Headache	Lavender
	Quartz Crystal
Heart	Agate
	Amethyst
	Aquamarine
	Aventurine
	Bloodstone
	Calcite
	Dioptase
	Garnet
	Gold

Heart- Con't	Haematite
	Heliodore
	Jade
	Jasper
	Kunzite
	Malachite
	Rhodonite
	Rhodochrosite
	Ruby
	Sapphire
	Silver
	Sugalite
	Variscite
Humility	Sardonyx
Immune System	Amethyst
	Agate
	Jadeite
	Rhodonite
	Ruby
	Rutilated Quartz
Infections	Copper
Inflammations	Malachite
Insomnia	Amethyst
	Peridot
	Topaz
	Zircon
Inter-Personal Relationships	Citrine
Intestinal problems	Obsidian
	Peridot

Intuition	Indicolite
	Smoky Quartz
Jealousy	Carnelian
Kidney	Aquamarine
	Citrine
	Dioptase
	Kunzite
	Rose Quartz
	Rubellite
	Sapphire
Liver	Aquamarine
	Citrine
	Rubellite
Lungs	Agate
	Carnelian
	Jade
	Opal
	Pearl
	Topaz
	Turquoise
Lymphatic System	Sodalite
Meditation	Amethyst
	Azurite
	Fluorite
	Haematite
	Meteorite
	Moldavite
	Quartz Crystal
	Tourmaline
	Turquoise

Memory	Agate
	Carnelian
	Emerald
	Opal
	Pyrite
	Sapphire
Menstrual Disorders	Chrysocolla
	Jadeite
	Moonstone
Motivation	Carnelian
	Rhodochrosite
Muscles	Aventurine
	Jadeite
	Lepidolite
	Peridot
Negativity	Amber
	Aquamarine
	Carnelian
	Coral
	Indicolite
	Jade
	Kunzite
	Obsidian
	Onyx
	Pearl
	Quartz Crystal
	Rubellite
	Rutilated Quartz
	Smoky Quartz
	Tourmaline

Nerves/ Nervousness	Alexandrite Amazonite Amber Aquamarine Calcite Dioptase Gold Rhodonite Topaz Tourmaline Turquoise
Nose	Silver
Pancreas	Sodalite
Patience	Emerald
Peace	Alexandrite Chrysoberyl
Perspective	Amazonite Amber Azurite Bloodstone Chrysoprase Ivorite Jadeite Sapphire
Pineal Gland/ Pituitary Gland	Amethyst Celestite Dioptase Royal Azel Sodalite Quartz Crystal

Priority Setting	Chrysocolla
	Emerald
Reasoning	Chrysocolla
	Citrine
	Indicolite
Rejuvenate	Indicolite
Respiratory System	Rutilated Quartz
	Turquoise
Self Confidence	Azurite
	Bloodstone
	Calcite
	Chrysocolla
	Kunzite
	Pyrite
	Rhodochrosite
	Rhodonite
	Rutilated Quartz
	Sardonyx
	Smoky Quartz
	Tiger's Eye
	Topaz
	Tourmaline
	Zircon
Self Control	Calcite
	Lavender
	Onyx
	Sapphire
	Sardonyx
	Topaz

Sexual Problems	Chrysoprase
	Copper
	Garnet
	Silver
Skin Problems	Coral
Sleeping problems	See Insomnia
Spine	Alexandrite
Spiritual Awareness	Alexandrite
	Amethyst
	Aquamarine
	Azurite
	Celestite
	Diamond
	Dioptase
	Fluorite
	Indicolite
	Kunzite
	Kyanite
	Lavender
	Obsidian
	Purple Rainbow-
	Fluorite
	Pyrite
	Rubellite
	Sapphire
	Sodalite
	Sugalite
	Tourmaline
Spleen	Aquamarine
	Fluorite
	Haematite

Stomach	Obsidian
Stress (mental)	Amethyst
	Bloodstone
	Celestite
	Obsidian
	Pyrite
	Rose Quartz
	Topaz
Teeth	Fluorite
	Malachite
Throat	Silver
	Topaz
	Turquoise
Tiredness	Copper
Tolerance	Kunzite
	Lepidolite
	Moonstone
	Tiger's Eye
	Tourmaline
Toxicity	See Detoxification
Ulcers	Dioptase
Urinary Problems	Silver

7. Appendix

REFERENCE INFORMATION:

BOOKS

Crystal Healing - Edmund Harold
Penguin Books - ISBN 0 670 90527 5

Discover Crystals - Ursula Markham
The Aquarian Press - ISBN 1 85538 108 7

Dreams That Come True - Dr. D. Ryback Ph. D.
The Aquarian Press - ISBN 0 85030 833 X

Love is in the Earth Laying-on-of-Stones - Melody
Earth Love Publishing House - ISBN 0 9628190 1 8

Reaching For The Other Side - Dawn Hill
Pan Books - ISBN 0 330 27029 X

The Force - Stuart Wilde
White Dove International - ISBN 0 930603 00 1

The Healing Power Of Crystals - Magda Palmer
Arrow Books Ltd - ISBN 0 09 965800 3

The Story of Edgar Cayce
There is a River - Thomas Sugrue
A. R. E. Press - ISBN 87604 151 9

The Truth Vibrations - David Icke
The Aquarian Press - ISBN 1 85538 136 2

BOOKS - Con't

You and Your Aura - Joseph Ostrom
The Aquarian Press - ISBN 0 85030 549 7

MEDITATIVE DISKS AND TAPES

Synchronicity Foundation, Inc. Faber, Va, USA
Tel: (804) 361 2323
In Australia: P. O. Box 349, North Balwyn. Victoria. 3104.
Tel: (03) 859 8182

Tony O'Connor - CD's and Tapes
Distributed by:
Steve Parish Publishing Pty Ltd
P. O. Box 361, Paddington. 4064. Q'ld.
Tel: (07) 254 1914

Candles, Incense, Oils. - To be updated next release.

8. Index

AAA
Abrasions, 169
Absorbs Negativity, 36
Acceptance, 7, 169
Acidity, 169
Adrenal Glands, 169
Agate, 74
Aggression, 169
Alcoholism, 169
Alexandrite, 75
Alpha Waves, 51
Amazonite, 76
Amber (Succinite), 77
Amethyst, 78
Anaemia, 169
Anger, 169
Angina, 169
Anniversaries, 21
Anus, 169
Anxiety, 170
Aquamarine, 80
Arrays Of Crystals, 33
Arthritis, 170
Asthma, 170
Astral Projection, 170
Astrology, 20
Atlantis, 29
Attitudes, 8
Auditory Or Visual Reception, 66
Aura, 170
Aventurine, 82
Awareness Of Crystals, 26
Aztecs, 29
Azurite, 84

BBB
Bad Temper, 170
Balance, 170
Balance Direction (Crystals) For Females, Males, 44
Before Attempting Healing, 33
Beta Waves, 51
Bleeding, 171
Blockages, 41
Blood, Blood Circulation, 171
Blood Clots, Blood Pressure (High), (Low), 172
Bloodstone (Heliotrope), 85
Bones, Bone Joints, 172
Bowel, 172
Brain, 51, 172
Broken Heart, 173
Bronchitis, 173
Burying, 38

CCC
Calcification, 173
Calcite, 86
Calming, 173
Cancer, 173
Carnelian, 87
Cassiterite (Tinstone), 89
Causing The Crystal To Move, 42
Celestite, 90
Chakra Balancing, 41, 42
Chakra #, Location, Name, 44
Chakra Opening, 173
Chakra Points And Relevant Details, 44, 45, 46
Chalcedony, 91
Channelling, 17, 22, 67, 173
Channelling Crystals, 29
Characteristics, 163

Chest, 173
Chrysoberyl, 92
Chrysocolla, 93
Chrysoprase, 94
Circulation, 174
Citrine, 95
Clairvoyance, 22
Clarity, 174
Clean All Gems Before And After Use, 35, 36
Closing Your Energy Centres, 41
Cluster Cleansing, 37
Colon, 174
Color In Our Make Up, 50
Communication, 29
Completely Clear, 33
Completely Cloudy, 33
Composite Vibratory Rate, 50
Concentration, 174
Copper, 96
Coral, 97
Corundum, 98
Courage, 174
Creativity, 174
Crystal & Gemstone Therapy, 68
Crystal & Minerals - Definitions, 28
Crystal Healing, 15
Crystal Master, 17
Crystal Mineral Water, 61
Crystal That Carries "Our" Ray, 50
Crystals, 6, 28
Crystals And Gems - Cleansing Methods, 36
Crystals Can Heal, 69
Cuts & Bruises, 175

DDD
Daily Meditation, 52
De Facto Home, 37
Death, 175
Deficient In A Specific Color, 50
Delta Waves, 51
Depression, 175
Despair, 175
Details On Minerals, 20
Detoxification, 175
Develop A Healing System, 69
Diabetes, 175
Diamond, 99
Digestion, 175
Dioptase, 101
Dis-Ease, 41
Disharmony, 176
Divination, 22, 59
Dowsing,22, 40, 48
Dreams, 8, 9, 54, 176

EEE
Ear Trouble, 176
Ectoplasm, 66
Edgar Cayce, 8
Egyptians, 29
Elixir, 61
Emerald, 102
Emotional Disturbances, Trauma 41
Emotional Insecurity, 176
Emotions, 63
Empowerment, 18
Ending Meditation, 57
Endocrine System, 176
Energy, 176
Energy Centres, 22

Enhancing Psychic Powers, 29
Entry Of Negative Energy, 47
Excess Energy, 19
Expectations, 8
Eyesight, 176

FFF
Feldspar, 104
Female Characteristics, 33
First Directive Received, 20
Fluoride, 36
Fluorite, 105
Forgiveness, 177

GGG
Garnet, 106
Gem Elixir, 61
Gemstones, 21, 44
Genes, 8
Getting Your Own Crystal/Gemstone, 35
Glands, 44, 177
Gold, 107
Grief, 177
Guardian Angels, 14
Guides, 10, 40

HHH
Haematite, 108
Headache, 177
Healing Point Of View, 28
Healing Will Take Place, 33
Healing., 69
Heart, 177
Heart Chakra, 14
Heliodore, 109
History Of Crystals, 29

Humility, 178
Hyacinth, 155

III
Immune System, 178
Incense, 38
Indicolite, 110
Individuals Color, 50
Infections, 178
Inflammations, 178
Insomnia, 178
Instinctive Knowledge, 16
Inter-Personal Relationships, 178
Intestinal Problems, 178
Intuition, 8, 23, 63, 179
Ivorite, 111

JJJ
Jade (Jadeite), 112
Jasper, 113
Jealousy, 179

KKK
Karma, 8, 22
Kidney, 179
Kundalini, 22
Kunzite, 115
Kyanite, 116

LLL
Lapis Lazuli, 117
Lavender, 119
Lemuria, 29
Lepidolite, 120
Listen To Your Inner Self, 72
Liver, 179

Lungs, 179
Lymphatic System, 179

MMM
Malachite, 121
Male Characteristics, 33
Master Healers, 33
Meditation, 40, 179
Mediums, 66
Memory, 180
Menstrual Disorders, 180
Meteorite, 122
Method Of Healing, 16
Mineral Water - (Gem Elixir), 61
Minerals, 6
Minerals Other Than Quartz, 34
Moldavite, 123
Moonstone, 124
Mother Of Pearl, 128
Motivation, 180
Moulded By Spirits, 66
Muscles, 180
Mystical, 12

NNN
Negative Energy, 36
Negativity, 180
Nerves, 181
New Age Of Crystals, 30
Nose, 181

OOO
Obsidian, 125
Ocean Or A Stream, 37
Onyx, 126
Opal, 127

Organs Of The Body, 41
Our Own Spitir Guides, 53

PPP
Pancreas, 181
Past Events, Past Lives, 14, 17
Patience, 181
Peace, 181
Pearl/Mother Of Pearl, 128
People Can See Auras, 63
Peridot, 129
Personal Level Of Expertise, 72
Perspective, 181
Physical Illness Or Dis-Ease, 41
Pineal Gland, 181
Pituitary Gland, 181
Points That Link The Various Bodies, 41
Popping Into My Head, 20
Power Sources, 29
Principal Point Of Connection, 42
Programmed Information, 29
Programming Crystals, 40
Psychic Awareness, 51
Psychic World, 11
Purple Rainbow Fluorite, 130
Pyrite, 131

QQQ
Quartz Crystal (Clear), 132
Quartz Family, 6, 28

RRR
Re-Cleanse All Your Gems, 37
Receptive Individuals, 10
Reincarnation, 65
Respiratory System, 182

Rhodochrosite, 134
Rhodonite, 135
Riverstone, 136
Rock Salts, 36
Rose Quartz, 137
Rotating A Group Of Stones, 61
Rotating Clockwise, 43
Rubellite, 138
Ruby, 139
Rutilated Quartz, 141
Rutile, 141

SSS
Salt Bath, 36
Sapphire, 142
Sardonyx, 144
Sea Water, 36
Selecting An Appropriate Stone, 35
Self Confidence, 182
Self Control, 182
Send It All Your Love, 33, 40
Seven Main Chakras, (Energy Centres), 41
Sexual Problems, 183
Significance Of Each Gem, 59
Silver, 145
Simplest Healing, 33
Single Spirit Channeller, 67
Skin Problems, 183
Sleeping Problems, 183
Slowing Down Your Brain Waves, 52
Smoky Quartz, 146
Sodalite, 147
Sound, 44, 50
Spine, 183
Spirit, 10, 13
Spirit Guide, 14, 67

Spleen, 183
Stomach, 184
Stress, 184
Subconscious Mind, 13
Sugilite, 148

TTT
Teacher Crystals, 29, 40
Teeth, 184
The Aura., 63
The Emotional Body, 63
The Etheric Body, 63
The Mental Body, 63
The Subconscious Body, 63
The Zodiac, 21, 163
Theta Waves, 51
Throat, 184
Tiger'S Eye, 149
Tiredness, 184
Tolerance, 184
Topaz, 150
Tourmaline, 151
Toxicity, 184
Transmitter Crystals, 29, 40
Turquoise, 153

UUU
Ulcers, 184
Unconscious Mind, 13, 64
Urinary Problems, 184
Using Crystals In A Healing Way, 24

VVV
Variscite, 154
Velocity Of The Crystal, 42
Vibratory Rates, 41

WWW
What Is The Purpose, 11
Which Body Is Affecting The Crystal, 42

YYY
Yes/No Responses, 48
Your Various Bodies, 14

ZZZ
Zircon, 155
Zodiac Dates, Signs, 163